ECCE ROMANI

Student's Companion 1

Prepared by The Scottish Classics Group

Oliver & Boyd

This Companion Book was prepared by the following members of the Scottish Classics Group:

Mary S. R. Burns	Assistant Deputy Principal and formerly Principal Teacher of Classics in The Mary Erskine School, Edinburgh
Andrew Kilgour	formerly Principal Lecturer in Classics, Jordanhill College of Education, Glasgow
Jessie G. Knox	formerly Principal and Principal Teacher of Classics, Hutchesons' Girls' Grammar School, Glasgow
Iain R. Macaskill	Principal Teacher of Classics, Knox Academy, Haddington
M. Barclay Miller	formerly Depute Rector and Principal Teacher of Classics, Perth Academy
Richard M. Orr	Adviser in Classics, Glasgow Division, Strathclyde Region
Henry L. Philip	formerly HM Inspector of Schools and Headmaster, Liberton High School, Edinburgh
William F. Ritchie	formerly Depute Rector and Principal Teacher of Classics, Arbroath High School
Kenneth G. Silver	formerly Rector, Jedburgh Grammar School, and Principal Teacher of Classics, Falkirk High School.
Geoffrey Suggitt	formerly Headmaster, Stratton School, Biggleswade, and Principal Teacher of Classics, George Watson's College, Edinburgh

Contents

Introduction

Exercenda	**Aenigmata**
Derivanda	**Ludi**
Memoranda	**Fabricanda**
Miranda	

What do these Latin words mean?

You will note that many of them end in **-nda**. The basic meaning of this sort of word is "things to be done". For example, **agenda, addenda** and **corrigenda** (words commonly used in English) mean "things to be discussed", "things to be added" and "things to be corrected."

Exercenda ("things to be practised") are exercises to practise your Latin.

Derivanda ("words to be derived"): This section deals with the study of how words in English (and in other languages) have been derived from Latin words and also how Latin words themselves are built up.

Memoranda ("things worth remembering") are famous Latin sayings, mottoes, proverbs, songs, and lines of poetry.

Miranda ("things to be wondered at") — a kind of "Curiosity Corner".

Aenigmata (from which English derives the word "enigma") are puzzles of various kinds.

Ludi are games you may wish to play.

Fabricanda ("things to be made") — plans and instructions for making models.

Unit I (Chapters 1–5)

Exercenda   1 *Select the correct word(s), write the whole sentence in Latin, and translate it into English:*

(a) viri Romani aestate in villis _____ .	habitat/clamant/habitant
(b) _____ defessae sub arbore _____ .	pueri/puellae; dormit/dormiunt
(c) in agris multi _____ _____ .	puellae/amicae/servi; laborat/laborant
(d) _____ infirmus _____ quod _____ est.	servi/servus; gemit/gemunt; defessa/defessus
(e) puella magna voce _____ quod _____ _____ .	cadit/cantat/clamant; laeti/laeta; est/sunt
(f) ubi servus ex agris ad villam _____ , laetus _____ .	redit/ridet/rident; dormit/dormiunt
(g) puer mane in horto _____ solus. iratus _____ .	ambulat/ambulant; est/sunt
(h) cur viri non _____? _____ quod solliciti _____ .	ridet/rident; gemit/gemunt; est/sunt

2 *Select the correct words, write the Latin sentence out in full, and translate it into English:*

(a) puella _____ amat; puer _____ amat.	stola/stolam; toga/togam
(b) pueri _____ infirmum ascendunt. subito cadit _____ . puellae _____ audiunt.	ramus/ramum; rami/ramus; fragor/fragorem
(c) _____ defessi, ubi _____ vident, _____ sunt.	pueri/puellae; villae/villam; laeta/laeti
(d) puer, ubi _____ conspicit, furtim appropinquat et _____ vexat.	puella/puellam; eum/eam
(e) quod amici _____ sunt, _____ petunt et ascendunt.	strenuus/strenuae/strenui; arbor/arborem
(f) puella _____ audit. clamor _____ puellam terret.	clamor/clamorem; magnus/magnum

3 *Select and translate:*

aestate multi (**servus/servi**) in agris et in villis (**laborat/laborant**). saepe servi (**gemit/gemunt**) quod defessi sunt.   Davus est (**servus/servum**).   hodie in horto (**laborat/laborant**).   Sextus appropinquat et (**Davus/Davum**) vexat.   (**Davus/Davum**) Sextum non amat.   iratus igitur "abi, moleste puer!" (**clamat/clamant**).   brevi tempore Cornelius et Aurelia (**appropinquat/appropinquant**). (**Cornelia/Corneliam**) sub arbore vident. "quid faciunt Marcus et Sextus?" clamat Cornelius. "(**suntne/estne**) in horto pueri?" subito (**puer/puerum**) in arbore conspicit, sed (**Marcus/Marcum**) non videt quod, dum Sextus (**arbor/arborem**) ascendit, Marcus in horto adhuc (**dormit/dormiunt**).

Derivanda

A medieval monk in his **scriptorium**.
(Photo: The Mansell Collection)

Words that are borrowed and adapted from another language are called "derivatives". Both words, **derivanda** and *derivatives*, come from the basic Latin word **derivare**, which itself illustrates very well the whole process of change and development in the shape and meaning of words. The Latin verb **derivare** started off from **de** ("from") + **rivus** ("stream", "watercourse") and meant in turn "to draw off water", "to divert a stream", "to turn something in a new direction" and "to derive one word from another."

It is estimated that roughly sixty per cent of all words in the English language are of Latin origin. Some Latin words were absorbed into the native language during the centuries of the Roman occupation of Britain. The coming of Christianity to Britain added words associated with the Church, and the Norman Conquest brought in numerous French words (of Latin origin) dealing with law and government. In the sixteenth century, the Renaissance further increased the number of Latin words assimilated into English.

Your knowledge of Latin, therefore, should help you build up a better understanding of the English language.

1 *Here are some English words derived from Latin words. Relate each English word to a Latin word you know:*

picture	brevity	cantata	vicinity
amicable	nominate	spectator	irate

6

2 *Using words from the pools below, complete the following table, matching the related Latin word and the correct meaning to each of the English words:*

Latin word	English word	Meaning
tempore	temporary	lasting a short time
_____	laboratory	_____
_____	furtively	_____
_____	solitude	_____
_____	vexation	_____
_____	dormitory	_____
_____	infirmary	_____
_____	conspicuous	_____
_____	multitude	_____

solus	conspicit	annoyance	large crowd
multi	laborat	easily seen	place for sick people
tempore	dormit	workshop	sleeping-quarters
infirmus	vexat	loneliness	lasting a short time
furtim		stealthily	

3 *Some Latin words have come into English without any change of form or meaning. These are known as "loan words", and many of them retain their Latin plural when used in English. Write down the Latin plural form of the following loan words:*

antenna	stimulus	vertebra	larva
cactus	narcissus	locus	bacillus
radius	gladiolus	formula	fungus

4 *The following Latin words are also found in English. What do they mean in Latin? Using a dictionary, if necessary, find out whether the meaning is different in English.*

villa   habitat   ego   multi-   piscina

Miranda

1 Bulla

The Latin word **bulla**, originally meaning "bubble", came to be used of anything which was bubble-shaped, e.g. a door-knob or pin-head, but especially the luck-charm worn by all free-born Roman children.

Its later meaning "seal" gave rise to the word "bull", e.g. a Papal Bull — an official document issued by the Pope and guaranteed as genuine by the Pope's seal attached to it.

Eventually, "bull" itself changed to "bill", meaning any written document, e.g. a Bill laid before Parliament.

2 Tandem

The literal meaning of the Latin word **tandem** ("at length") has been jokingly extended to mean "lengthwise", referring to two persons or objects (e.g. cyclists, horses, machines, etc.) one behind the other. In recent years, the use has been extended even more. Where one person is going to follow or succeed another in an important post, it is quite common to have them working "in tandem", i.e. both doing the same job, one learning it from the other.

A tandem bicycle. (Photo: W. R. Pashley Ltd)

3 Cave!

The Latin imperative **cave** was taken over into school slang with the spelling (and pronunciation) "cavey", meaning "keep a look out for those in authority (i.e. the teachers)."

A mosaic from Pompeii.
(Photo: The Mansell Collection)

Aenigma

Short dashes indicate word-endings, not separate words. The solution is on page 95.

Clues across

2 cur tu semper puer molestus _____ , Sexte? (2)

4 _____ in arbore sedet? (4)

7 Flavia est amica mea.   quis est amicus _____ ? (4)

9 puer _____ magnam furtim petit. (7)

13 hodie _____ puellae in horto ambulant. (4)

15 estne Marcus puer magnus? _____ vero! (3)

16 ex agris ad vill _ _ currunt servi. (2)

17 ego vocem magnam audio.   quid tu _____ ? (5)

18 cur _____ in hortum non venis, Marce? (2)

19 magnum fragor _ _ puellae audiunt. (2)

20 ubi Flavia in horto ambulat, Cornelia _____ conspicit. (3)

22 puellae Sextum non _____ . (5)

25 "cur tu _____ semper vexas?" clamat Davus. (2)

26 _____ Sextus arborem ascendit, Marcus eum sollicitus spectat. (3)

27 tunica est brevis, _____ est longa. (4)

Clues down

1 Sextus magna voce _____ . (6)

2 magnam vocem _____ magnum fragorem puella audit. (2)

3 puellae _____ arbore sedent. (3)

4 _____ hodie ambulas, Cornelia? (3)

5 cave, Sexte!   ramus est infirm _ _ . (2)

6 servi _____ agris laborant. (2)

8 ego togam amo.   tu stolam _____ , Cornelia. (4)

10 _____ infirmum Sextus non videt. (5)

11 ubi Sextus ex arbore cadit, Davus _____ . (5)

12 Marcus est puer Romanus.   _____ Romanae sunt Cornelia et Flavia. (5)

14 quod Sextus est molestus, Davus _____ non amat. (3)

17 Cornelia et Flavia sunt puell _ _ . (2)

21 "Flavia est amica _____ " clamat Cornelia. (3)

22 puella _____ hortum currit. (2)

23 Cornelia amic _ _ in agris conspicit. (2)

24 quod defessae sunt, ad villam lente ambula _ _ . (2)

Unit II (Chapters 6–8)

Exercenda

1 *Match each Latin word with its English meaning. The first one is done for you.*

(a)	nuntius	ix	(i)	he hands over
(b)	ignavus	____	(ii)	greetings!
(c)	petit	____	(iii)	always
(d)	appropinquat	____	(iv)	they fear
(e)	igitur	____	(v)	cowardly
(f)	statim	____	(vi)	he wishes
(g)	subito	____	(vii)	immediately
(h)	lente	____	(viii)	he approaches
(i)	prope	____	(ix)	a messenger
(j)	semper	____	(x)	slowly
(k)	faciunt	____	(xi)	he(she) reads
(l)	salve!	____	(xii)	he(she) makes for
(m)	tradit	____	(xiii)	cool
(n)	timent	____	(xiv)	therefore
(o)	terrent	____	(xv)	near
(p)	vult	____	(xvi)	they are doing
(q)	inquit	____	(xvii)	suddenly
(r)	legit	____	(xviii)	they frighten
(s)	frigidus	____	(xix)	warm
(t)	calidus	____	(xx)	he(she) says

2 A Playlet in Two Scenes

Dramatis Personae: Marcus et Sextus, duo pueri
Cornelia et Flavia, duae puellae
Cornelius, senator Romanus
Aurelia, uxor eius

Scaena prima: in atrio
(intrant pueri et puellae)

CORNELIA: cur tu rides, Flavia? ego non rideo, nam necesse est ad urbem redire.

FLAVIA: rideo quod Sextus ad urbem redit. me vexare semper vult.

SEXTUS: semper timetis, tu et Cornelia! puellas non amo. nolo ad urbem redire. ego volo in villa manere, per agros errare, arbores ascendere, in rivo natare.

MARCUS: age, Sexte! nondum necesse est ad urbem redire. hodie hic manemus. ego volo in silvam ambulare. visne venire?

CORNELIA ET FLAVIA: nos quoque venire et in ripa sedere volumus. servos in agris laborantes videre amamus. neque lupos neque canes timemus.

(exeunt pueri et puellae)

Scaena secunda

(in atrium intrant Cornelius et Aurelia)

CORNELIUS: eheu! nuntius me ad urbem revocat. princeps omnes senatores consulere vult. iam necesse est multas epistolas scribere et omnia parare.

AURELIA: ita vero! si statim redire vis, strenue laborare necesse est. Davus servos celeriter excitare potest.

(exeunt Cornelius et Aurelia. intrant puellae. Flavia lacrimat.)

FLAVIA: Sextus est puer molestus. eum non amo quod semper me vexat. me in rivum trahere vult; sed ego natare non possum; perterrita sum.

CORNELIA: noli timere, Flavia! iam tu es salva. si prope me manes, Sextus te vexare non potest. age! dies iam est calidus. volo in horto sub arbore sedere. visne venire?

(exeunt puellae ridentes)

canis, a dog   **noli timere!** do not be afraid!

3 *List TEN present infinitives from the previous passage and translate them,*

e.g. **redire,** to return

4 *With help from the same passage, translate into Latin:*
(a) Flavia is afraid of dogs and wolves.
(b) Sextus wishes to walk into the wood and to climb trees.
(c) The girls like to sit under a tree in the garden.
(d) Cornelius does not remain in the villa, for the emperor wishes to consult him.

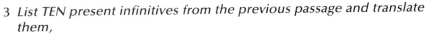

5 *Read the following story and answer the questions below. Do not translate unless asked to.*

Cornelia in atrio sola sedet. Flavia advenit et "volo" inquit "te ad meam villam ducere." Cornelia laeta "eugepae!" clamat, "sed necesse est Aureliam consulere."

Aurelia "nolo" inquit "te solam per agros errare, Cornelia, sed hodie Davus non laborat. Davus te et Flaviam ad villam Flavianam ducere potest." Davus, quem pueri saepe vexant, Corneliam amat; sed hodie est iratus quod vult in villa sedere.

brevi tempore ad villam Flavianam adveniunt. dies est calidus et prope rivum frigidum puellae laetae ludunt. eheu! brevi tempore necesse est redire.

Davus et Cornelia per silvam ambulant. subito fragorem audiunt. perterritus Davus lupum magnum conspicit. "cave, Cornelia!" clamat; sed, dum Davus lupum repellere parat, lupus Corneliam petit. Cornelia clamat perterrita. sed quid audiunt? ecce! Marcus et Sextus adveniunt et ad lupum currunt. iam pueros lupus petit. Cornelia salva est. Davus ramum arripit et tandem lupum repellit.

(a) Why was Cornelia **laeta**?
(b) Why did Aurelia send Davus with the girls?
(c) What were Davus' normal feelings towards (i) the boys, (ii) Cornelia?
(d) Which phrase tells you why Davus was not pleased to go?
(e) Where did the girls play? Which words suggest this was an appropriate place?
(f) Whom did the wolf try to attack first?
(g) What turned it away?
(h) Who finally drove off the wolf?
(i) How would Davus feel towards the boys after this?
(j) Does this story change your impressions of Sextus?

Derivanda

1 Prefixes and suffixes extend and modify the meanings of words. A prefix is attached to the beginning of a word, a suffix to the end. You have already met Latin verbs with the prefixes

> **re-** (or **red-**) meaning "back", "again"
> **ad-** meaning "to"

e.g. **redit** : he goes back **revocat** : he calls back
repellit : he drives back **adveniunt** : they come to

Other common prefixes are: **e-** (or **ex-**) meaning "out"
in- (or **im-**) meaning "in" or "into"

What would the following verbs mean?

exit	adit	reveniunt
adducit	expellit	impellit
recurrit	educit	invocat

2 The Latin word **hostis** means "an enemy". The English adjective "hostile" means "like an enemy." Give single English words for:

(a) like a man
(b) like a boy
(c) like a slave

The Latin word **deus** means "a god." From it we get the English verb "to deify" meaning "to make into a god." Give single English words for:

(a) to make bigger
(b) to make (someone) afraid
(c) to divide into branches

Can you explain why the English word "qualify" comes to mean what it does?

Memoranda

1 Latin Mottoes

Since Latin is a very concise and pithy language, it still has world-wide currency as the language for mottoes, coats of arms, etc. Even when local languages replaced Latin within the former Roman Empire during the Middle Ages, Latin continued (and still continues to this day) as an international language. Latin mottoes coined in the past are still all around us, and new ones continue to be invented.

Each Latin word can carry a great deal of meaning, and words like **est** or **sunt** which can be easily supplied from the context are often omitted. For example, in the phrase **in vino veritas** the word **est** is understood; but, even when such words are added, a word-for-word translation will not always bring out all of the meaning packed into the Latin, and so "There is truth in wine" implies much more than the mere words. It means that, when a person drinks too much wine, he is liable to blurt out the truth unintentionally and say things which he would tactfully keep to himself when sober.

Try to work out the meaning of the following phrases in which **sum, es, est** or **sunt** has to be supplied:

ubi tu Gaius, ego Gaia.	Marriage vow of Roman bride
ars longa, vita brevis.	Saying of Hippocrates, founder of medicine
gloria finis.	Family motto
montani semper liberi.	Motto of West Virginia
bis pueri senes.	Latin proverb
vox populi, vox dei.	Advice given to the Emperor Charlemagne

ars, skill, art	**liber,** free
vita, life	**bis,** twice
finis, end, aim	**senes,** old men
montani, mountain–dwellers	**populus,** people

2 *A Carol*

Dormi, Iesu

dormi, Iesu! mater ridet,
quae tam dulcem somnum videt.
dormi, Iesu, blandule!
si non dormis, mater plorat;
inter fila cantans orat.
blande, veni, somnule!

dulcis, sweet	**blandule,** peacefully	**cantans,** singing
somnus, sleep	**plorat,** she weeps	**orat,** she prays
somnulus, sleep	**inter fila,** while spinning	**blandus,** gentle, soothing

Polish Carol Melody

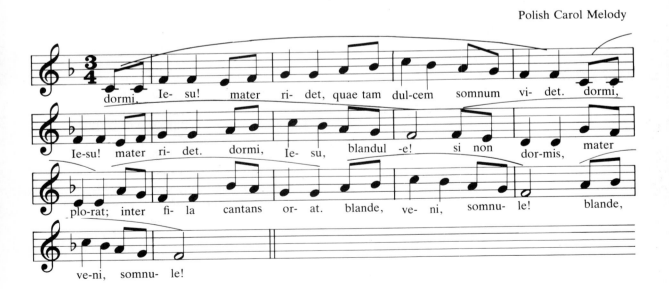

Aenigma

Clues across

3 you (*sing.*) are getting up
6 you (*sing.*) love
7 are you (*sing.*) watching?
10 she hears
12 you (*pl*) are
14 you (*sing.*) are
15 he remains
17 we are
18 you (*sing.*) are carrying

The solution is on page 95.

Clues down

1 Hello! (*sing.*)
2 we have
4 you (*sing.*) go in
5 come on! (*sing.*)
7 we rise
8 she goes out
9 they are sitting
11 you (*sing.*) fear
12 to be
13 I swim
16 she is

Unit III (Chapters 9–12)

Exercenda

1 (a) *From the pool of words below select an appropriate verb to complete the following sentences. Copy out the sentences and translate them. Do not use the same word twice.*

   (i) pater et mater Marci in villa _____ .
   (ii) Davus iratus servos in hortum _____ .
   (iii) Aurelia ancillas in atrium _____ .
   (iv) senatores in urbem _____ .
   (v) novi servi in agris _____ .

convocat	iubent
veniunt	festinant
sedent	habitat
reprehendit	laborant
mittit	venit
verberat	currunt

(b) *Complete the endings and translate the sentences:*

   (i) ancillae cistas in raed__ coniciunt.
   (ii) in urb__ Marcus togam gerit.
   (iii) duo equi in are__ stant.
   (iv) mox raedarius eos excitat.   in vi__ festinant.
   (v) servi in agr__ effugiunt.

2 *Complete the columns below:*

	Present Infinitive	Group Number	Meaning of Infinitive
rogamus	rogare	1	to ask
mittit	mittere		
coniciunt	conicere		
iubeo			
reprehendo		3	
impedimus	impedire		
stat			
habemus			
discedimus	discedere		
portant			

3 *Change one of each pair of words to the genitive to form a phrase.*
Combine this phrase with the words in the right-hand column to form
a sentence. Translate the sentence.

e.g. **puer** } est nova.
    tunica }

This becomes **tunica pueri** est nova. *The boy's tunic is new.*

(a) vilicus } pueros terret.
    baculum }

(b) Cornelius } patrem amat.
    filia }

(c) Cornelius } strenue laborat.
    filius }

(d) dominus } servos terret.
    ira }

(e) vox } Marcum excitat.
    mater }

(f) liberi } in raeda sunt.
    cistae }

(g) Marcus } cibum amat.
    amicus }

(h) canis } in via conspicimus.
    vestigia }

(i) ianitor } ad ianuam sedet.
    villa }

4 *Translate into English:*

(a) puer ignavus ad ripam rivi descendere non vult, nam natare nondum
    potest.

(b) cur nuntius prope ianuam villae sollicitus stat?   eum salutare nobis
    necesse est.

(c) pueri scelesti tacite appropinquant quod puellas, quae semisomnae
    sunt, terrere parant.

(d) cur vos ex villa domini tam furtim disceditis?   quo festinatis?
    vobis necesse est statim ad villam redire.

(e) servosne lupum repellere iubes, pater?   nos omnes perterriti sumus.

(f) servus defessus neque ridet neque cantat, nam Davus eum iubet in
    agris laborare.

(g) eo ipso tempore mater Marci cubiculum puerorum intrat et irata "cur
    non surgitis?" clamat.

5 Translate into English:

Poor Coachman!

hodie Cornelius amicum visitare parat, qui in urbe vicina habitat. servi igitur occupati sunt. Davus, ubi in aream venit, omnes servos strenue laborare iubet. alii cistas ex villa portant, alii eas in raeda ponunt. etiam raedarius est occupatus, nam equos in area curat.

subito servi magnam cistam in raedam magno fragore coniciunt. raedarius equos sollicitus spectat. equi, quod sunt perterriti, ex area ad agros currunt. raedarius eos revocare temptat, sed nihil facere potest.

interea servi in area adhuc stant. servos raedarius iratus spectat et, "cur cistas in raedam conicitis?" inquit. "cur equos meos terretis? cur non tacite laboratis? Gaius Cornelius brevi tempore discedere vult, sed nunc ego nullos equos habeo." servi tamen nihil respondent.

tum Cornelius ipse appropinquat et raedarium miserum reprehendit. "cur servos terres, sceleste? cur equos tuos non petis? mihi discedere tempus est. festina!"

raedarius per agros ad silvam festinat, ubi equi sub arboribus errant. dum equos ex silva ad raedam lente ducit, servos ridentes audit.

Derivanda

1 *Explain the meaning of the English words derived from the Latin words shown opposite them.*

   (a) **habitare** : habitation, inhabitant
   (b) **curare** : curator, incurable
   (c) **observare** : observation, observant
   (d) **spectare** : spectator, spectacle
   (e) **temptare** : attempt, temptation

2 *Study the list of English adjectives along with the Latin word (noun) from which they are derived. Give the meaning of the English word:*

English word	Latin word	Meaning of English word
paternal maternal fraternal	pater mater frater	
equine canine lupine	equus canis lupus	

18

3 There are many English words which end in "-able" or "-ible," e.g. "portable" (from **portare**), "able to be carried." Think of the Latin word from which these English words come and give the meaning of the English word:

English word	Latin word	Meaning of English word
habitable tenable excitable legible reprehensible audible		

4 European languages which are direct descendants of Latin are called Romance languages, the most familiar being French, Italian and Spanish. Here are some examples of how Latin words now appear in these languages:

Latin	French	Italian	Spanish
pater	père	padre	padre
mater	mère	madre	madre
filius	fils	figlio	hijo
filia	fille	figlia	hija
frater	frère	fratello	(hermano)
soror	soeur	sorella	(hermana)

(N.B. The Spanish words for "brother" and "sister" — "hermano" and "hermana" — are derived from the Latin words **germanus** ("brother") and **germana** ("sister").)

Memoranda

1 What do these mottoes mean?

(a) Family mottoes:
semper paratus   semper victor
semper fidelis   cave lupum! (Wolfe family)
labora!   cave! Deus videt. (Cave family)
audio sed taceo

(b) Other mottoes:
semper eadem   (Queen Elizabeth I)
cave canem!   (An RAF squadron)
cave leopardum!   (An RAF squadron)
ecce ancilla Domini   (A girls' school)
audi! vide! tace!   (United Grand Lodge of Freemasons)

fidelis, faithful

2 One of the more fruitful sources of the poems which we shall be introducing is the poet Martial (or, to give him his full name, Marcus Valerius Martialis) who lived from AD 40 to about AD 104. He was a Spaniard who came to live in Rome. There, he wrote a series of short poems called *Epigrams*. These poems, ranging from two to about thirty lines in length, give us a vivid and witty picture of Roman society at that time, covering all moods from biting satire to gentle compassion.

Translate these two epigrams:
(a) The first example we have chosen is about Tongilianus and his remarkable nose:

> Tongilianus habet nasum; scio, non nego. sed iam
> nil praeter nasum Tongilianus habet.

Martial, Epigrams XII.88

scio, I know   **nego,** I deny   **nil praeter,** nothing but

(b)   non amo te, Sabidi, nec possum dicere quare.
       hoc tantum possum dicere, non amo te.

Martial, Epigrams I.32

nec, and . . . not   **quare,** why   **tantum,** only
dicere, to say   **hoc,** this

A story is told of Thomas Brown who was a student at Oxford University in the seventeenth century. He was threatened with expulsion for unacceptable behaviour, but the Head of his College, Dr Fell, offered him a reprieve if he could translate the above Epigram. This is the translation he produced:

> I do not love thee, Dr Fell;
> The reason why I cannot tell;
> But this I know, and know full well,
> I do not love thee, Dr Fell.

Miranda   PUNCTUATION

The ancient Romans were very conscious of sentence structure, but they did not give the reader much help with punctuation between clauses or even between sentences. This must have given the Roman reader no end of trouble, what with the flexible word order of Latin and the mistakes which even the best of copyists could make from time to time. Even in English, the absence of commas can be crucial to the understanding of a sentence, as can be seen in the old school-boy rhyme:

> Caesar entered on his head
> A helmet on each foot
> A sandal in his hand he had
> His trusty sword to boot.

The word "punctuation" is derived from the Latin word **punctum.** Originally, **punctum** meant a dot or point made in a wax tablet, but over the centuries it graduated to the status of a full stop.

Other punctuation signs began their lives simply as abbreviated Latin words, e.g. **quaestio** (meaning "a question") was shortened to ⊗ and **io** (meaning "hurray!") to ǒ . These are printed now as **?** and **!** respectively.

In the writings of the ancient Romans themselves, abbreviations and even entire private shorthands were not uncommon. Cicero's freedman and secretary, Tiro, is credited with the invention Ƹ (= **et**) which has become our symbol & (= "and"). Alphabets printed in children's schoolbooks long ago in Britain contained the symbol & after the letter Z. To make it clear that this symbol was distinct from the alphabet itself, the following words were inserted after Z — "and per se &", giving rise to the modern word for the symbol & — "ampersand."

Aenigma   Jobs and relationships

Find the Latin words which suit the clues below. Words are in a straight line (horizontal, vertical or diagonal, but never backwards). Draw a line round each word as you find it. The first one has been done for you.

	a	b	c	d	e	f	g	h	i	j	k
1	P	R	I	N	C	E	P	S	T	U	V
2	A	D	V	I	L	I	C	U	S	R	O
3	F	N	O	P	E	G	O	X	A	A	S
4	E	L	U	M	A	N	G	O	N	E	S
5	N	I	A	N	I	T	O	R	C	D	O
6	S	B	T	M	T	N	E	S	I	A	R
7	S	E	R	V	I	I	U	R	L	R	O
8	P	R	A	M	I	C	U	S	L	I	R
9	F	R	A	T	E	R	A	S	A	U	E
10	U	S	E	N	A	T	O	R	E	S	S

1 slaves	8 female friend	15 you (*sing.*)
2 master	9 driver	16 you (*pl*)
3 overseer	10 emperor	17 we
4 father	11 servant girl	18 senators
5 wife	12 door-keeper	19 parent
6 messenger	13 slave-dealers	20 sisters
7 male friend	14 I	21 brother

The solution is on page 95.

21

Unit IV (Chapters 13–16)

Back at the Villa

dum Cornelii ad urbem iter faciunt, Davus servos in aream convocat. "agite!" inquit. "iam necesse est in agros festinare et ibi strenue laborare." alios servos in vineas, alios in agros mittebat. multi in oliveta ibant.

in agris servi boves ducebant, boves plaustra trahebant, plaustra onera magna ferebant. in olivetis servi quidam arbores ascendebant et olivas baculo petebant. cuncti diu et strenue laborabant. septima hora defessi sub arboribus quiescebant. mox in agris laborabant usque ad noctem.

ubi iam advesperascebat, murmur rotarum audiunt. ecce! appropinquat cisium. in cisio sedet vir togam gerens.

"salve, domine!" clamat Davus. "quis es tu?"

"ego sum senator Romanus," respondet vir. "villam Gai Cornelii peto."

"ecce villa Cornelii!" respondet Davus. "Cornelius ipse tamen abest. iter Romam facit cum uxore et liberis. fortasse raedam eius in Via Appia vidisti."

"raedam...? raedam...?" mussat vir. "ita vero! in Via Appia erat raeda — sed in fossa immobilis. quot in Cornelii raeda erant?"

Davus "septem in raeda iter faciebant — Cornelius et Aurelia uxor eius, Eucleides paedagogus, Syrus raedarius, tres liberi — duo pueri et una puella."

"ita vero!" inquit vir. "tres viri, tres liberi, una femina in via stabant. non procul stabat tabellarius quidam; fortasse eius culpa Cornelii raeda in fossa erat."

Davus sollicitus "cur ad villam nunc venis?" rogat.

"Neapolim iter faciebam" respondet vir, "sed iam advesperascit et mei equi sunt defessi. volo hic pernoctare, nam amicus Cornelii ego sum."

Davus statim servos convocat et "ferte cibum equis!" clamat. "ancillae, cubiculum parate! amicus Cornelii in villa pernoctare vult."

servi cibum, ancillae cubiculum parabant, sed Davus "eheu!" gemebat. "hic amicus domini mei in villa pernoctare potest; sed ubi pernoctat dominus meus? fortasse in caupona, fortasse in fossa!"

usque ad (+ *acc.*), right up to
vidisti, you saw

paedagogus, -i (*m*), tutor
equis, for the horses

Derivanda

1 *Complete the blanks to form English words derived from the Latin:*

pes, pedis : ped _ _ , ped _ _ _ _ _ _ n
dominus : domin _ _ e, domin _ _ t, domin _ _ n
tardus : tard _ , _ _ tard
decimus : decim _ _ , decim _ _ e
custodio : custod _ _ n, custod _

2 *Give the meaning of these Latin words as they are used in English, and use each one in an English sentence to bring out its meaning:*

rota   janitor   murmur   via   onus   vim

3 *From which Latin words are these English words derived?*

civil   apparent   partial   fatuous
ferocity   pulverise   frustration revenue

4 *Use your Latin to explain the meanings of the words in italics:*

(a) There will be a *simultaneous* broadcast of the Queen's speech on all channels.
(b) *Auxiliary* groups will be at hand if they are required.
(c) The *itinerary* you have chosen will be difficult, but interesting.
(d) There is not a *vestige* of truth in her story.
(e) My brother cannot make up his mind; he keeps on *procrastinating*.

5 *Connect each of these English words with a Latin numeral and explain their meanings:*

(a) unit   (c) trio   (e) dual
(b) octave   (d) sextet   (f) duel

6 *Relate the names of the following months to the Latin numerals. Do you notice anything odd?*

      September   October   November   December.

7 Here are examples of how Latin numerals now appear in some modern languages:

	Latin	French	Italian	Spanish
1	unus, -a, -um	un, une	uno, una	uno, una
2	duo, duae, duo	deux	due	dos
3	tres, tria	trois	tre	tres
4	quattuor	quatre	quattro	cuatro
5	quinque	cinq	cinque	cinco
6	sex	six	sei	seis
7	septem	sept	sette	siete
8	octo	huit	otto	ocho
9	novem	neuf	nove	nueve
10	decem	dix	dieci	diez

Memoranda

1 The boredom of learning arithmetic tables is not new. This is how Augustine felt about the way they chanted them when he was at school:

unum et unum duo, et duo quattuor, odiosa cantio erat.

odiosus, -a, -um, hateful, unpleasant

2 **civis Romanus sum:** St Paul is said to have made this claim when he was accused. How did this claim affect the way he was treated? (Acts 25, 11–12)

3 **Pater noster:** The opening of the Lord's Prayer.

This has become a single word in English — paternoster — and it has several meanings:
(a) a rosary;
(b) every tenth (large) bead on the rosary, when the Lord's Prayer is recited;
(c) anything strung like a rosary, e.g. a fishing line on which a series of small hooks is strung at intervals;
(d) a lift consisting of a series of platforms attached to a continuously moving cable; passengers enter it while it is still moving.
There is also a street in London called Paternoster Row.

This Latin word-square has been found
at several Roman sites, including
Cirencester in England, where it
was scratched on a house wall:

```
S AT OR
A R E P O
T E NE T
OP E R A
R OT A S
```

Whether you start at the top left and work along and down, or at
the bottom right and work left or upwards, you find the same
message:

sator (The sower) **Arepo** (Arepo) **tenet** (holds) **rotas** (the wheels)
opera (with work, i.e. carefully).

This may appear a clever but rather meaningless sentence. However,
it is thought that the word-square contains a Christian cryptogram.
The letters, at any rate, can be rearranged in the form of a cross,
leaving four letters which also have a special significance, if translated
into Greek letters, Alpha (A) and Omega (Ω), the first and last in the
Greek alphabet.

If you need any help to understand the Greek reference, see The
Revelation of St John Chapter 22, verse 13.

The same word-square has been found near the River Euphrates and at
two places in Pompeii.

The letters of **pater noster** can also be read in another clever way to
form a different type of cross:

Miranda   ROMAN NUMERALS

(a) The Roman number system depends on certain key numbers which are used as base numbers:

Arabic number	Roman number
1	I
5	V
10	X
50	L
100	C
500	D
1000	M

I stands for one finger, II for two fingers, III for three fingers.

V represents the shape made by the thumb and first finger.

X is formed by placing one V on top of another, thus $\overset{V}{\wedge}$

C` stands for the Latin word **centum** ("a hundred").

M stands for the Latin word **mille** ("a thousand").

D is half of M when it is written ⏀ or CⅠⅅ

There are several theories about L. One is that it is derived from the signs (⅃ and ⊥) used in inscriptions for 50; another is that it is half of C when written ⌐ .

(b) Rules for calculating numbers:

(i) When a "smaller" number appears at the right-hand side of a "bigger" number, the smaller is added to the larger, e.g. VI = V + I (i.e. 6) and CXII = C + X + I + I (i.e. 112).

(ii) When a "smaller" number appears at the left of a "bigger" number, the smaller is subtracted from the larger, e.g. IV = V − I (i.e. 4) and XC = C − X (i.e. 90).

Roman milestones. Can you spot the Roman numbers? (Photo: The Mansell Collection)

(c) The main difficulty in using the Roman system was that bigger numbers took up so much space. The Arabic system avoids this problem by having a symbol for 0. The same digits can have different values since it is their position which shows whether they are units, tens, hundreds, thousands, etc. Compare the Arabic numbers 33, 303 and 3033 with their Roman equivalents XXXIII, CCCIII and MMMXXXIII.

(d) The Roman system is still in use today. For example, Roman numerals are often used to number chapter headings of books, and you will see them on the faces of many clocks and on certain buildings and monuments. Look out for them also on television where they indicate the dates of films and other programmes. Find examples of Roman numerals in your home and in your locality. Join with the others in your class to see how many different uses you can find.

Big Ben, which rises above the Houses of Parliament. (Photo: Popperfoto)

1 *Write down the Latin words for the following and give their English equivalents:*

IV   III   X   IX   C   M   XI   VI   VIII   V

2 *Give the English equivalent of the following numerals:*

XV	XX	XIX
CL	XL	XIV
LXVII	LX	XVI
MCMLXXXVIII	MLXVI	MCDXCII

¹	²	³	⁴	⁵	⁶	⁷			
⁸			⁹		¹⁰			¹¹	¹²
¹³		¹⁴		¹⁵		¹⁶	¹⁷		
¹⁸						¹⁹			
		²⁰						²¹	
²²		²³	²⁴				²⁵		
		²⁶		²⁷		²⁸	²⁹		
³⁰			³¹		³²			³³	
	³⁴		³⁵		³⁶				
³⁷		³⁸							

Lines indicate whole words, short dashes indicate endings only. *(The solution is on page 95.)*

Clues across

1 rustici _____ sunt quod lupus boves petit.   (5)

6 Davus non est _____ Romanus.   (5)

8 princeps _____ ad urbem revocat.   (3)

9 Aurelia mult _ _ ancillas habet.   (2)

10 Roma est _____ magna.   (4)

13 estne Sextus puer temerarius? _____ vero!   (3)

16 ubi raeda parata est, servi cum _____ appropinquant.   (4)

18 Cornelius iratus _____ reprehendit.   (9)

20 dum servi raedam parabant, Cornelius et Aurelia in villa _____.   (8)

22 quando clamores puerorum _____ ?   (8)

25 ego togam amo; _____ stolam amat.   (2)

26 duo _____ tres sunt quinque.   (2)

27 raeda quattuor rotas, cisium duas _____ habet.   (6)

30 pueri _____ quod Cornelius epistolas scribit. (6)
32 virgam mihi _____ , Dave! (4)
34 nobis necesse est _____ agros ad villam ambulare. (3)
35 servi gemebant quod magna _____ portabant. (5)
37 dum Davus in horto laborabat, _____ spectabam. (3)
38 cave Sexte! in ramo _____ sedes. (7)

Clues down

1 quod dies est calidus, in villam _____ vult. (5)
2 quando murmur _____ audiebas, Marce? (7)
3 Davus servos iubet cist _ _ ad raedam portare. (2)
4 plaustra sunt vehicula _____ . (5)
5 lupum bacul _ _ repellunt. (2)
6 servi tarde in agros ambulabant; puer celeriter _____ . (8)
7 Cornelia ad villam Flavianam _____ vult. (3)
11 ego _____ civis Romanus. (3)
12 ubi Cornelii parati sunt, raeda per _____ ibat. (6)
14 puellae sunt defess _ _ . (2)
15 raedarius cum equis in via _____ . (5)
17 puellae, _____ in pictura vides, sunt Cornelia et Flavia. (4)
19 quod nox appropinquabat, Cornelii ad cauponam _____ . (5)
21 videbas _ _ illud cisium, Marce? (2)
22 raedarius magna _____ equos agebat. (4)
23 quattuor et sex sunt _____ . (5)
24 Cornelii _____ ad urbem faciebant. (4)
28 cur Sextus _____ vexat, Cornelia? (2)
29 duos pueros et _____ puellam in horto video. (4)
31 Cornelia rivum timet, nam natare _____ potest. (3)
33 _____ arborem ascendere non timebam. (3)
36 nos sumus cives Romani; _____ servi sunt. (2)

2 *The Riddle of the Sphinx*
   quid est animal quod prima luce quattuor pedibus, meridie duobus,
   vesperi tribus se movet?

          meridie, at mid-day   **vesperi,** in the evening

   The solution is on page 95.

29

Unit V (Chapters 17–19)

Exercenda

1 *From the pool of words below select an appropriate adjective to complete each sentence. Pay regard to case, number, gender and sense. Write the sentence in full and translate it.*

(a) caupo _____ subito ad ianuam apparuit.

(b) Aurelia et Cornelia cubitum ire volebant, nam valde _____ erant.

(c) eheu! in lecto _____ pernoctare nolo.

(d) pueri cubitum ire nolebant. viatores _____ videre volebant.

(e) cauponam _____ prope Viam Appiam invenire non potestis.

(f) canes _____ Corneliam non terrebant.

(g) pueri _____ fuerunt quod ad mediam noctem vigilabant.

(h) Cornelius valde sollicitus erat ubi raedam _____ in fossa videbat.

(i) semper est _____ in caupona pernoctare.

(j) raeda _____ in fossa haeret.

obesus	magni	omnes	bonam
parvus	laetos	meliorem	periculosum
defessus	noster	sordidam	scelestum
defessa	defessae	magnos	nostra
parva	immobilis	laeti	immobilem
bonas	sordido	bonum	sordidum

2 *Complete the following table:*

	Singular		Plural	
Person	Present	Perfect	Present	Perfect
1	neco	necavi	necamus	necavimus
3	audit	audivit	audiunt	
2	mittis	misisti	mittitis	
3	vigilat		vigilant	vigilaverunt
1	maneo		manemus	mansimus
2	habes		habetis	habuistis
1	rideo	risi	ridemus	
1	volo	volui	volumus	
2	potes	potuisti	potestis	
1	eo	ivi	imus	

30

3 *From the parts of the verb given in column 1, deduce in each case the first three Principal Parts and give the meaning of the Present Infinitive:*

Column 1		1st sing. Present	Present Infinitive	1st sing. Perfect	Meaning of Pres. Infin.
clamat	clamavit	clamo	clamare	clamavi	to shout
apparemus	apparuimus				
habes	habuisti				
petunt	petivisti				
ducimus	duxerunt				
dolemus	doluerunt				
surgunt	surreximus				
respondet	respondisti				
timemus	timuerunt				
vitas	vitavistis				

4 *The adjectives in brackets are all in the nominative singular. Make them agree with the nouns in gender, case and number.*

militem (Romanus)   viros (omnis)
cauponarum (parvus)   cauponum (laetus)
cenas (bonus)   lectis (magnus)
principum (iratus)   viatores (*acc.*) (defessus)
homini (omnis)   patre (meus)

5 *Translate:*

(a) Cornelii filia multa nomina praeclarorum civium in epistola legit.

(b) ancilla timida ossa in fossa invenit.

(c) multa cubicula in villa erant.

(d) magna onera plaustra in oliveta nostra portant.

(e) ex area magna vehicula traxerunt equi.

(f) quamquam puella timida pericula timebat, in caupona pernoctavit.

31

Derivanda

1 Many English words are formed from the stem of a Latin noun (i.e. the genitive singular, minus the genitive ending), e.g.

	Stem	English word
ars, artis aqua, aquae tempus, temporis nomen, nominis	art- aqu- tempor- nomin-	artistic aquatic temporary nominate

Find the stem of the following Latin nouns and form English words from the stem:

	Stem	English word
hospes, hospitis onus, oneris fabula, fabulae nox, noctis bos, bovis miles, militis ager, agri		

2 Give the Latin noun (with meaning) from which these English words are derived:

pedal itinerant urban culpable numerous vocal rotary partial	pes, pedis	foot

3 Give the meaning of the compound verbs in columns 2, 3 and 4:

1	2	3	4
portare :	importare	reportare	exportare
ponere :	exponere	imponere	reponere
ducere :	reducere	educere	inducere
currere :	recurrere	praecurrere	excurrere
mittere :	immittere	emittere	praemittere

4 The prefix **in-** (which may become **im-**, **il-** or **ir-** depending on the consonant which follows) sometimes has a negative force, e.g.

audible : able to be heard
inaudible : not able to be heard.

Give the opposites of:

explicable	curable	responsible
possible	visible	revocable
legible	movable	hospitable

5 *Here are some Latin words which are used in English. Check in your dictionary to see which plural form is used. Is it the Latin plural, the English plural, or both?*

rota   circus   stadium   campus   arena   medium
syllabus   terminus   appendix   hippopotamus   formula

Memoranda

Translate these Latin sayings:

1 **ecce homo!:** These were the words used by Pontius Pilate to the people (St John's Gospel 19.5) when Jesus was seen wearing the crown of thorns. Pictures of Jesus wearing the crown of thorns are usually given this title.

2 **ego et meus rex:** This was how Cardinal Wolsey began his letters in the King's name to monarchs of other countries. This is the normal word order in Latin, so why did Henry VIII object to it?

3 **non Angli, sed angeli:**   These words are said to have been used by Pope Gregory the Great when he saw the fair-haired English captives (Angles) being sold as slaves in Rome.

4 **non omnia possumus omnes** (Virgil): Some word like **facere** must be understood with **possumus**.

5 **possunt quod posse videntur** (Virgil): This is the motto of Worcester College of the Blind.

6 **non possumus:** This was the reply of Pope Clement VII to Henry VIII when he was petitioned by the latter to allow him to divorce Catherine of Aragon. The Latin phrase is now used in English to mean "a refusal".

7 **quod potui, perfeci:** Family motto

    quod, what   **perfeci,** I did

Miranda

Sometimes Latin words and phrases are abbreviated and become English words in their own right, with no obvious connection with Latin:

1 Did you know that, when the sheriff gathers a "posse", he is using a form of Latin? The word **posse** is an abbreviation of the phrase **posse comitatus,** in which the meaning of the infinitive has been extended from "to be able" to the idea "power".   **comitatus** is a genitive, meaning "of the county." A "county" was originally the area controlled by a count, a companion (Latin **comes, comitis**) of the king.

2 The word "mob" (disorderly crowd) comes from the Latin **mobile vulgus.** The noun **vulgus** means "crowd" and **mobilis** is the opposite of **immobilis; mobile vulgus** therefore means "the fickle crowd."

3 A slang word for "clothes" is "togs". This comes from the Latin **toga.**

4 "Bus" is an abbreviation of **omnibus** ("for all" i.e. a vehicle for transporting everyone). The following amusing poem was written earlier this century by A. D. Godley, showing what the different case endings of **motor bus** might have been. (N.B. The Latin words in the poem are pronounced as if they were English words.)

Motor Bus

What is this that roareth thus?	Whither shall thy victims flee?
Can it be a **motor bus?**	Spare us, spare us, **motor be!**
Yes, the smell and hideous hum	Thus I sang; and still anigh
Indicat motorem bum!	Came in hordes **motores bi;**
Implet in the Corn and High	**et complebat omne forum**
Terror me motoris bi.	**copia motorum borum.**
Bo motori clamitabo	How shall wretches live like us
Ne motore caedar a bo!	**Cincti bis motoribus?**
Dative be or Ablative	**Domine, defende nos**
So thou only let us live.	**Contra hos motores bos!**

impleo (2), to fill	**copia, -ae** (*f*), large numbers
clamitabo, I shall shout	**cinctus, -a, -um,** surrounded
ne caedar, so as not to be killed	**hos,** these
compleo (2), to fill	

N.B. The Corn (Market) and High are two streets in Oxford.

5 Inscriptions provide fascinating and immediate contact with the past. They survive in surprisingly large numbers, despite damage from weathering and vandalism, and provide a unique source of contemporary information about Roman life. Extant examples range from imperial proclamations and personal epitaphs to lovers' effusions and election slogans on the walls of Pompeii.

   The following lament (**querela, -ae** (*f*)) is engraved (**sculpo, -ere** (3), to engrave) on one of the pyramids in Egypt by a sister mourning her dead brother:

   vidi Pyramidas sine te, dulcissime frater,
   et tibi, quod potui, lacrimas hic maesta profudi
   et nostri memorem luctus hanc sculpo querelam.

sine (+ *abl.*), without	**profudi,** I shed
dulcissimus, -a, -um, dearest	**nostri memorem luctus,** as a
quod potui, all that I could do	memorial of my grief
maestus, -a, -um, sad	**hanc** (with **querelam**), this

	a	b	c	d	e	f	g	h	i	j	k
1	I	A	I	I	M	T	T	D	U	X	I
2	U	I	U	U	I	I	V	I	H	D	T
3	S	F	U	D	S	V	S	X	A	I	I
4	S	M	I	S	I	S	T	I	B	X	M
5	I	V	U	A	S	V	I	T	U	I	U
6	S	I	V	I	T	I	E	T	I	S	E
7	T	R	A	X	I	T	M	R	M	T	R
8	I	I	V	I	S	T	I	U	U	I	U
9	S	M	A	N	S	I	M	U	S	N	N
10	C	L	A	M	A	V	E	R	U	N	T

Find the words which have the following meanings:

1 she said
2 they feared
3 you (*sing.*) sent
4 you (*pl*) sent
5 we ordered
6 they have shouted
7 I sent
8 he has ordered
9 she went
10 you (*sing.*) spoke
11 we have remained
12 I went
13 they have heard
14 I have been
15 he has seen
16 I led
17 he dragged
18 you (*sing.*) have gone
19 we have had
20 you (*pl*) ordered
21 she has ordered

Words are in a straight line (horizontal, vertical or diagonal, but never backwards). Draw a line round each one as you find it.

The solution is on page 96.

Unit VI (Chapters 20–22)

Exercenda

1 *In each group, one verb is the "odd man out" because it is different from the others in number or person or tense. Write down the "odd men out" and give the reasons for your choice:*

(a) inspexisti, rides, rogant, timent

(b) parant, misimus, petimus, dicunt

(c) possum, audiebamus, ibam, volebamus

(d) volebant, puniverunt, surreximus, manebant

(e) extraxisti, vidimus, diximus, surgitis

(f) faciebas, eo, nonvis, sum

(g) sumus, tradidistis, respondemus, dedimus

(h) eras, inspiciebas, volebam, nolui

(i) fuerunt, vidit, ivit, erant

(j) voluistis, poteras, nolebas, respondisti

2 *The words in brackets are in the nominative case, singular or plural. Keeping the same number, change these words to the dative case and translate the sentence:*

e.g. viatores (**urbs**) appropinquant.
    viatores urbi appropinquant. *The travellers approach the city.*

(a) nuntius epistolam (**senatores**) statim tradidit.

(b) Eucleides fabulas multas (**pueri**) narrare vult.

(c) nonne tu omnia (**pater tuus**) dixisti?

(d) mandata (**ancillae**) dare semper amabamus.

(e) quis pecuniam (**miles**) dare poterat?

(f) vir stolam (**uxor molesta**) tradere nolebat.

(g) servi ignavi (**domina irata**) nihil respondebant.

(h) dominus equos (**caupo et servi**) tradit.

3 *Look for clues to help you decide whether the word in bold type is dative or ablative, and then translate the sentences:*

(a) ingentia onera ad villam **plaustro** trahebat.

(b) hospes mortuus **amico** in somnio apparuit.

(c) **magno silentio** noctis perterritus erat.

(d) caupo **viatoribus** "valete!" exclamavit.

(e) pueri lupum **clamoribus** terruerunt.

(f) multa et mira **pueris** narravit.

(g) servi boves **virgis** verberabant.

(h) Cornelius **raedario misero** "o sceleste!" inquit. "tua culpa raeda est in fossa."

(i) ubi necesse fuit **Cornelio** discedere, vilicus multa **domino** promisit.

(j) tempus est urbem **armis** non **auro** servare.

arma, -orum (*n.pl*), arms, weapons

4 *Opposite each of the words, give its gender, number, case and meaning; in the last two columns, write the form of* (a) **magnus** *and* (b) **ingens** *which agrees with the noun.*

	Gender	Number	Case	Meaning	magnus	ingens
rotam raedas clamore lupum arbori baculum corporum urbi aedificia	feminine	singular	accus.	wheel	magnam	ingentem

(The tables on pages 9 and 35 of *Ecce Romani* Book 2 will help you, if necessary.)

5 *Translate:*

(a) omnes urbis viae erant plenae hominum, mulierum, servorum.

(b) nobis necesse erat praedonibus pecuniam tradere.

(c) baculo ingenti mercatorem miserum verberavit praedo.

(d) senatores, ubi ad portas urbis advenerunt, clamores hominum iratorum audire poterant.

(e) una mulierum mihi omnia narravit; ego statim eadem meo patri dixi.

(f) duo pueri, ubi ex horto in villam cucurrerunt, tunicas sordidas ancillis tradiderunt.

(g) nobis licebat aut in villa manere aut in agros villarum vicinarum cum amicis ambulare.

(h) orator, nomine Cicero, multa senatoribus dicebat, multa civibus.

mulier, -eris (*f*), woman
praedo, -onis (*m*), robber
eadem, the same story
aut ... aut ..., either ... or ...

6 *Translate, and then explain why these tenses of the verb were used:*

   (a) ubi Cornelii ad urbem advenerunt, Titus eos ad Portam Capenam exspectabat.

   (b) quamquam pecuniam bene custodiebamus, praedones eam arripuerunt.

   (c) Sextus, quod lupum timebat, auxilium statim petivit.

   (d) iam advesperascebat ubi ad cauponam advenerunt.

   (e) postquam laborem finivit, sub arbore quiescebat.

   (f) ubi nuntius atrium intravit, quid faciebat Cornelius?

   (g) Sextus de fabula militis cogitans diu vigilabat, sed tandem obdormivit.

   (h) princeps, quamquam uxorem valde amabat, aurum ei tradere noluit.

   (i) quamquam Davus servos in agros ire iussit, servi laborare nolebant.

   (j) urbi iam appropinquabant ubi Marcus subito "ecce sepulcrum!" clamavit.

Derivanda

1 *Many English nouns are formed from the supine of Latin verbs.*
Complete the tables, following the example given:

Latin verb	Supine	English word
(a) **narro** exclamo invenio video extraho trado mitto pono	**narratum**	**narration**

(b) **specto** audio narro conduco invenio curo inspicio ago	**spectatum**	**spectator**

2 *Complete the following English words derived from Latin:*

finio (4)   fin _ _ , fin _ _ _

primus, -a, -um   prim _ , prim _ _ _

civis, civis (*m*)   civ _ _ , civ _ _ , civ _ _ _ _ _

urbs, urbis (*f*)   urb _ _ , suburb _ _

bene   bene _ _ _ , bene_ _ _ _ _ _

3 *Use your Latin to explain the meaning of the words in bold type:*

   (a) The cavalry were sent out on a **punitive** expedition.

   (b) Some people are against **corporal** punishment.

   (c) At Easter, Christians celebrate the **Resurrection** of Jesus.

   (d) I have no **pecuniary** interest in that business.

   (e) That political party has no **mandate** to carry out such a policy.

Memoranda

1 *The following mottoes and proverbs use the dative case. What do they mean?*

   (a) ignavis semper feriae.

   (b) hodie tibi, cras mihi.

   (c) Gloria in excelsis Deo.

   (d) Deo, patriae, amicis.

   (e) Deo gratias.

   (f) non nobis solum.

   (g) iustitia omnibus.

   (h) urbi et orbi.

   (i) non nobis sed omnibus.

   (j) non nobis, Domine.

> **feriae, -arum** (*f.pl*), holidays
> **in excelsis,** in the highest
> **patria, -ae** (*f*), native land
> **gratiae, -arum** (*f.pl*), thanks
>
> **solum,** alone
> **iustitia, -ae** (*f*), justice
> **orbis, orbis** (*m*), world

2 *Match the Latin sayings with their English equivalents:*

   (a) quieta noli movere!

   (b) qui tacet consentire videtur.

   (c) de mortuis nil nisi bonum.

   (d) vox et praeterea nihil.

   (e) multae manus onus levius faciunt.

   (f) festina lente!

   (g) ferre ligna in silvam.

> **consentire,** to agree
> **levius,** lighter
> **lignum, -i** (*n*), log

Many hands make light work.	Speak no ill of the dead.
To carry coals to Newcastle.	Let sleeping dogs lie.
He's all mouth.	Silence means consent.
More hurry, less speed.	

Adeste, Fideles!

Adeste, Fideles,
   Laeti triumphantes!
Venite, venite in Bethlehem!
   Natum videte
   Regem angelorum!
Venite, adoremus Dominum.

   Stella duce, Magi
   Christum adorantes
Aurum, thus et myrrham dant munera.
   Iesu infanti
   Corda praebeamus.
Venite, adoremus Dominum.

   Cantet nunc hymnos
   Chorus angelorum;
Cantet nunc aula caelestium.
   Gloria
   In excelsis Deo.
Venite, adoremus Dominum.

natus, -a, -um, born	**munus, -eris** (*n*), gift
rex, regis (*m*), king	**corda praebeamus,** let us give our hearts
adoremus, let us worship	**cantet,** let (it) sing
stella duce, led by a star	**aula, -ae** (*f*), court

Miranda   WHAT A WORD!

The derivatives of **corpus, corporis** (*n*), a body, include:

corpus	corporeal
corporal	corps
corporation	corpse
corpulent	corselet (from the old spelling of
corpuscle (**corpusculus** =	corpse — "corse")
"a little body")	corset
corporate	corsage

The most outlandish of derivatives from **corpus** is said to have originated in the first three words of consecration in the Roman Catholic Mass — **hoc est corpus.** This proved unintelligible to some worshippers who did not understand Latin, and it ultimately joined the English language as "hocus-pocus."

Aenigma A "Tense" Word Search

Find the 1st person singular of the Present, Imperfect and Perfect tenses of the following verbs:

esse	habere	sumere
dare	ire	trahere
dicere	manere	venire
ducere	mittere	

Words are all in a straight line — vertically, horizontally or diagonally.

Letters may be used more than once when one word cuts across another, but a word cannot be contained completely within another word, e.g. **sumo** cannot also provide **sum**.

Draw a line round each word as you find it.

The solution is on page 96.

	a	b	c	d	e	f	g	h	i	j	k	l
1	M	A	N	S	I	R	D	E	D	I	O	V
2	I	T	R	A	H	O	O	I	I	E	B	E
3	S	U	M	P	S	I	D	U	C	O	V	N
4	I	S	U	M	O	H	A	B	E	O	E	I
5	D	U	C	E	B	A	M	O	B	I	N	O
6	S	D	I	X	I	B	T	R	A	X	I	D
7	U	T	R	A	H	E	B	A	M	F	E	U
8	M	I	T	T	E	B	A	M	X	U	B	X
9	E	I	V	I	H	A	B	U	I	I	A	I
10	B	D	A	B	A	M	A	N	E	O	M	B
11	A	S	U	M	A	N	E	B	A	M	H	A
12	M	I	T	T	O	V	M	S	E	R	A	M

41

Unit VII (Chapters 23–25)

Exercenda

1 *In each of the following pairs, identify the future tense and write it down with its meaning:*

   (a) surgemus, movemus   (e) dicet, licet
   (b) sedent, ponent   (f) eram, inveniam
   (c) coniciunt, poterunt   (g) fertis, videbitis
   (d) eritis, itis   (h) manes, ages

2 *Complete the following table:*

Pres. Infin.	Group No.	Meaning	Present	Future	Pluperfect
mittere currere ridere adiuvare posse pervenire conicere ferre dare iubere agere	3	send	mitto	mittam	miseram

3 *For each of the following verbs, write down the person, number and tense and then translate:*

e.g. dabitis: 2nd Person, Plural, Future = you (*pl*) will give

discedebant	occurram	coniciunt	constitues
stas	itis	advenient	manes
conspicietis	erunt	veneratis	posuerant
volueramus	potueram	induunt	exspectabit
dabunt	manebas	ascenderas	fecisti

4 *Match each Latin verb with its correct translation. The first one is done for you.*

   (a) tacebamus   viii   (i) you send
   (b) verberavisti   ____   (ii) they had given
   (c) dices   ____   (iii) she saw
   (d) traditis   ____   (iv) they were
   (e) poterunt   ____   (v) you will say
   (f) clamabant   ____   (vi) I saw
   (g) vidit   ____   (vii) they were able
   (h) videt   ____   (viii) we were silent

(i)	mittitis	____	(ix)	you will throw
(j)	dederunt	____	(x)	you have beaten
(k)	mittetis	____	(xi)	you are handing over
(l)	dederant	____	(xii)	they gave
(m)	volebam	____	(xiii)	they will be able
(n)	poterant	____	(xiv)	we had ordered
(o)	erunt	____	(xv)	they shall be
(p)	eunt	____	(xvi)	I used to want
(q)	conicies	____	(xvii)	she sees
(r)	videbam	____	(xviii)	you will send
(s)	fuerunt	____	(xix)	they kept shouting
(t)	iusseramus	____	(xx)	they go

5 *Translate:*

(a) cras servi cenam parabunt; cenam cum amicis sumemus.

(b) nos sub arbore sedebimus; Eucleides in hortum veniet et libros ad nos feret. nos libros non legemus.

(c) cur virum non audietis? nisi audietis, alios docere non poteritis.

(d) quando equos ad rivum ducere poterunt? ego equos ducere non possum quod pluit.

(e) miles per multa pericula nos omnes duxerat; nihil timebat.

(f) servi cistas in domum ferent. ancillae cistas in atrio inspicient.

(g) ubi liberi cras erunt? tu liberos non videbis, nam e domo hodie mane exibunt.

(h) si hodie iter facere volent duo pueri, nemo cum eis ire nolet.

(i) puella pecuniam fratri dederat; frater servum iusserat librum emere.

(j) quid servi in agris hodie facient? laborabuntne? minime! cur non hodie laborant? hodie sunt feriati, sed cras diligenter laborabunt. ita vero! cras servos in agris conspicies.

6 *Examine the verbs carefully. First decide the Group number since this will help you to get the tense right; then translate the sentences.*

(a) vilicus, quod dominus eum terret, omnia diligenter faciet.

(b) si amicus meus auxilium a civibus petet, princeps eum non puniet.

(c) quod magnum periculum timet, domina in cauponam non veniet.

(d) ad Curiam ire in animo habemus; lecticam igitur conducemus.

(e) ubi ad Circum ibunt, Corneliam domi relinquent.

(f) servos rem totam explicare dominus iubet, sed illi nihil respondent.

(g) habetisne satis pecuniae? ita vero! novem servos statim ememus.

(h) "quis auxilium principi feret?" "nemo principem adiuvare nolet, nam omnes cives eum valde timent."

(i) "quando ab urbe effugies?" "numquam urbem, quam semper amavi, relinquam."

(j) Sextus gaudet quod multa et mira in itinere conspiciet.

Derivanda

1 *Using the Latin words in the second column, try to deduce the meanings of the English words:*

English word	Derived from	Meaning of English word
traction	traho (3)	
tremor	tremo (3)	
furtive	furtim	
total	totus, -a, -um	
occurrence	occurro (3)	
relinquish	relinquo (3)	
repellent	repello (3)	

2 *Using the same approach as in Exercise 1, state the Latin words from which these English words are derived and give their meanings.*

English word	Derived from	Meaning of English word
mural		
reference		
agent		
library		
infinite		
aquatic		
arc		
purify		
transit		
nocturnal		

3 Prefixes: **de-,** down, away
  con-, com-, together
  trans-, tra-, across
Give the meanings of the following compound verbs:

convenire	componere	convocare	comportare
transire	transmittere	transferre	traicere
deponere	descendere	detrahere	decurrere

4 The Latin adjective **formosus** comes from the noun **forma, -ae** (*f*), meaning "beauty" and the adjective ending **-osus, -a, -um** which means "full of." **formosus** therefore means "full of beauty", i.e. "beautiful". What do the following Latin adjectives mean?

rimosus	verbosus	lacrimosus	fabulosus	silvosus
periculosus	numerosus	onerosus	pecuniosus	aquosus

If taken into English, the **-osus** ending becomes either "-ose" or "-ous". Which of the above Latin words have been treated in that way, and in which form do they appear?

Sometimes English creates its own words ending in "-ose" or "-ous", even though there is no Latin equivalent ending in **-osus**. What do the following mean?

amorous   impecunious   clamorous

5 *Use your knowledge of Latin to work out the meanings of the following Latin phrases as commonly used in English sentences:*

(a) Because he had not been given any warning, he had to make an **ex tempore** speech at the meeting.
(b) In an emergency, make for the nearest **exit**.
(c) After the stormy sea-crossing, they were all glad to be on **terra firma** again.
(d) The local side beat the visitors 5 goals to **nil**.
(e) People prefer to see wild animals in their natural **habitat** rather than in cages.
(f) 10 divided by 3 is 3.33333 **ad infinitum**.
(g) The club committee discussed **inter alia** the provision of lunches for members.
(h) The pathologist performed a **post mortem** on the victim of the accident.
(i) He did not beat about the bush but plunged straight **in medias res**.

Memoranda

1 *Translate the following sayings and mottoes which use the future tense:*

quis custodiet ipsos custodes? (Juvenal)

aut viam inveniam aut faciam. (school motto)

ascendam. (family motto)

Deus mihi providebit. (family motto)

in hoc signo vinces. (These words appeared to Constantine the Great in a vision in which he beheld the Cross.)

    vinco, vincere (3), **vici, victum**, to conquer

2 **o tempora! o mores!** "Oh, how times have changed!" (literally "O times! O customs!") — a famous statement made by the orator Cicero, who was shocked by the treacherous behaviour of Catiline the conspirator.

ipse dixit. (used of someone making a dogmatic assertion with no supporting evidence)

3 No change of profession for Diaulus!

      nuper erat medicus, nunc est vespillo Diaulus.
        quod vespillo facit, fecerat et medicus.
                      (Martial)

nuper, recently	**vespillo, -onis** (*m*), funeral-undertaker
medicus, -i (*m*), doctor	**et,** also
quod, what	

45

Miranda   **MUSICAL SIGNS — Some Notes for Musicians!**

The following is a list of note-shapes evolved in the Middle Ages, together with their Latin names. It begins with the sign for the longest note.

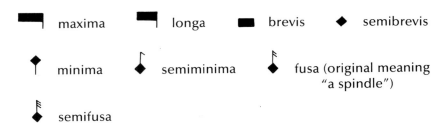

What do you think the Latin names mean?
What is the time-value of each sign in relation to its predecessor?
What signs have survived into modern times and what are their modern names?

Aenigmata   **1 Sights of Rome**

Find your way into the middle of the maze and then out again. Start at F on the left-hand side and emerge at A in the middle of the right-hand side. Move horizontally or vertically (never diagonally), using every letter once and only once. On the way, "go through" nine famous places in Rome. The clues tell you types of people whom you would associate with the places, and the numbers in brackets indicate the number of letters in the word(s). *The solution is on page 96.*

1 speakers (5)
2 athletes (6,7)
3 fighters (13,7)
4 drivers (6,7)
5 travellers (3,5)
6 booksellers (9)
7 guards (4,11)
8 senators (5)
9 litter-bearers (5,6)

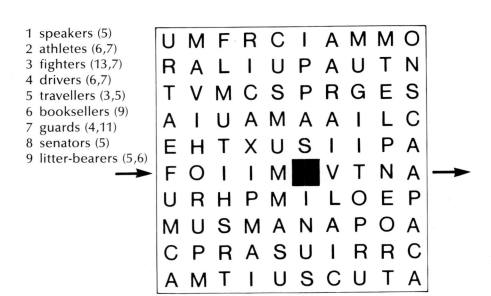

2 What's wrong here?

There are deliberate mistakes in this picture of a scene in ancient Rome. Make a list of them. You should be able to find twenty.

The solution is on page 96.

Unit VIII (Chapters 26–27)

Exercenda

1 *Identify the tense and translate:*

1 rogant	11 accusavisti	21 abibam
2 rogabant	12 coniciunt	22 respondet
3 rogabunt	13 conicient	23 respondit
4 rogaverant	14 coniciebant	24 videbis
5 habet	15 coniecerunt	25 habuerunt
6 habitat	16 scribam	26 dabo
7 trademus	17 custodiemus	27 cogitabamus
8 tradimus	18 apparuit	28 poterant
9 traxit	19 dedisti	29 poterunt
10 volebant	20 pluet	30 redierat

2 *In the left-hand column, insert the form of* **hic, haec, hoc** *which agrees with the noun in number, case and gender. In the right-hand column, use the appropriate form of* **ille, illa, illud**.

_____ urbem	_____ rebus
_____ onere	_____ lupum
_____ hominum	_____ domini (*nom.*)
_____ rerum	_____ dominae (*gen.*)
_____ mercatori	_____ sonitu
_____ die	_____ aedificium
_____ oculos	_____ milites (*nom.*)
_____ militis	_____ manui
_____ mater	_____ canum
_____ nomina	_____ capita

3 *For the following nouns, write the appropriate part of* (a) **hic** *and* (b) **ille**, *paying particular regard to gender, case and number:*

hic	ille	Noun
hae	**illae**	**silvae** (*nom.*) pedem mulierum multitudini sepulcris patris ianuarum corpus caupones (*acc.*) raedarii (*gen.*) diebus

4 *Fill in the blanks by changing the tenses of the verbs, but keeping the same person and number as the given form:*

Infinitive	Present	Imperfect	Future	Perfect	Pluperfect
habere				habuimus	
ferre	fert				
manere		manebatis			
scribere					scripserant
nolle	nonvis				
ire			ibunt		
ducere		ducebam			
venire				venisti	
posse					potuerant
esse	est				

5 *Translate:*

   (a) nonne longo itinere defessi estis?   nonne hic pernoctare vultis?
   (b) quid tibi illa nocte accidit?   cur hoc nobis non dixisti?
   (c) multa et mira in caupona audivimus.   tales fabulas iterum atque
       iterum audire volebam.
   (d) mittemusne alteram epistolam?   minime!   nova mandata vilico ipse dabo.
   (e) quod in via cecideram, manus sordidas aqua lavi.
   (f) parentes hanc pecuniam liberis dabunt;   filius ad ludos ibit;   filia
       librum emet.
   (g) patruus meus prima luce surgere solet, nam prope arenam sedere vult.
   (h) multas res civibus promiserat;   nihil tamen eis tradere in animo habebat.
   (i) licebitne mihi magnam ludorum partem spectare?
   (j) abhinc multos dies hos sonitus audiverat, ubi magnam servorum
       turbam conspexit.

6 *Translate:*

(a) ancillae cistas efferebant et in raeda imponebant.

(b) de raeda descenderat Cornelius et ad villam adibat.

(c) milites onera trans rivum transportaverunt;   nunc ad montes procedunt.

(d) ille senator clientes praecedebat ubi homo quidam ad eum accurrit.

(e) vilicus servum tunica arripuit et ad villam reduxit.

(f) ubi caupo in cubiculum irrupit, praedones bona hospitis deiecerunt et in aream effugerunt.

7   Husbands and Wives

Graeci antiqui, ut scriptores narrant, uxores filiasque domi retinere solebant;   raro mulieribus exire licebat.   viri Graeci uxores de rebus urbanis numquam rogabant, sed omnia in foro ipsi soli constituebant.

Romani tamen nihil tale faciebant.   verba uxorum diligenter audiebant.   una cum uxoribus in urbis viis ambulabant.   uxores etiam solas in urbem exire sinebant.   et viri et uxores apud liberos servosque magnam auctoritatem habebant.

Romani, ubi amicos ad cenam invitabant, uxores quoque horum amicorum saepe vocabant.   valde enim amabant uxores filiasque viri Romani.   itaque ille praeclarus historiae Romanae scriptor, Cornelius Nepos nomine, haec scribit: "quem Romanorum pudet uxorem in convivium adducere?"   at uxores, quamquam in conviviis aderant, raro in lectis sicut viri accumbebant, sed in sellis sedere solebant.   neque mulieribus saepe licebat vinum bibere; nam talia facere, ut Romanis videbatur, non erat decorum.

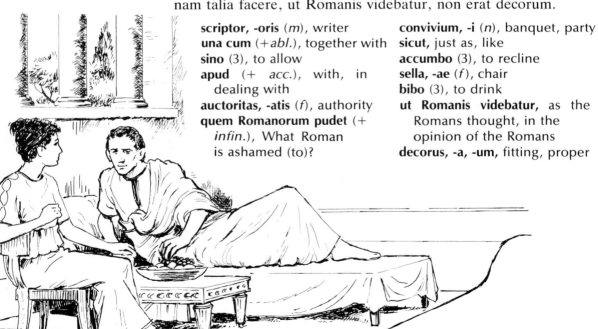

scriptor, -oris (*m*), writer
una cum (+*abl.*), together with
sino (3), to allow
apud (+ *acc.*), with, in dealing with
auctoritas, -atis (*f*), authority
quem Romanorum pudet (+ *infin.*), What Roman is ashamed (to)?

convivium, -i (*n*), banquet, party
sicut, just as, like
accumbo (3), to recline
sella, -ae (*f*), chair
bibo (3), to drink
ut Romanis videbatur, as the Romans thought, in the opinion of the Romans
decorus, -a, -um, fitting, proper

Derivanda

1 Complete the columns below by giving the Latin word(s) from which each English word is derived and the meaning of the English word:

English word	Latin word	Meaning of English word
custodian docile decapitate manual adjacent oculist exclude adhere aperture accident		

2 Some Latin verbs and their compounds are the source of many English derivatives. See how many English derivatives you can write down for each of the following:

    duco, ducere (3), duxi, ductum
    mitto, mittere (3), misi, missum
    fero, ferre, tuli, latum

3 Here are some more Latin phrases which are now in common usage in English. What do they mean?

   (a) When children are in school, teachers act **in loco parentis.**
   (b) The student received his degree **in absentia.**
   (c) He was determined to pay off his debts **in toto.**
   (d) The archaeologist examined his finds **in situ** before removing them to the museum.
   (e) Above the names of those who had been killed in the war appeared the words **In Memoriam.**
   (f) The hope is that the memory of these heroes will last **in perpetuum.**
   (g) She earned £3650 **per annum.** How much is that **per diem?**
   (h) They charged us interest at the rate of 9 **per cent(um).**
   (i) The footballer was suspended **sine die.**
   (j) The school received a **per capita** allowance of money to buy books and equipment for its pupils.

4 The word **res** is extensively used in Latin. For example, **res gestae** means "exploits" or "achievements" (literally "things which have been done"). What would be the meaning of **res bene gestae** and **res male gestae**?

   Can you suggest meanings for the following common Latin phrases?

   res Romana   **in medias res**
   res publica   **res urbanae**

5 For those who study French as well as Latin, the following notes should be helpful. Being a daughter-language of Latin, French shows a close resemblance to its parent in vocabulary. This resemblance is not always easy to recognise because of the changes which took place in the French language as it developed. For example, very often an "s" preceding another consonant at the beginning of a word becomes "e acute"; and the loss of an "s" within a word is shown by the circumflex accent,

e.g.
Latin	French	Meaning
sponsus	époux	bridegroom, spouse
magister	maître	master

Do you know the French words for the following English words? Even though you do not study French, you can look up an English-French dictionary to get the answers.

English word	Latin word	French word
school	schola (school)	
to write	scribere (to write)	
head	testa (roof tile, skull)	
backbone	spina (spine)	
star	stella (star)	
donkey	asinus (ass)	
clothes	vestimentum (garment)	
animal	bestia (beast)	
to taste	gustare (to taste)	
to reply	respondere (to reply)	
holiday	festum (holiday, festival)	
window	fenestra (window)	

6 Scientists use a form of shorthand to refer to the various elements, e.g.

Al	=	Aluminium	H	=	Hydrogen
C	=	Carbon	O	=	Oxygen
Ca	=	Calcium	I	=	Iodine

It is not difficult to see why these particular letters were chosen; but it is not always the first or first two letters that are chosen. Often, letters from Latin words (or words which have been made to look like Latin words) are chosen.
Can you match the three columns?

English words	Latin words	Chemical symbols
(1) silver	(a) plumbum	(i) Sn.
(2) gold	(b) cuprum	(ii) Na.
(3) tin	(c) ferrum	(iii) Ag.
(4) iron	(d) aurum	(iv) Cu.
(5) sodium	(e) stannum	(v) Au.
(6) lead	(f) nitra	(vi) Fe.
(7) copper	(g) argentum	(vii) Pb.

Memoranda

1 Natus est Rex Gloriae

The tune can be found in the *Oxford Book of Carols* No. 79 and in
The Church Hymnary (3rd Edition), Hymn 515.

> Quem pastores laudavere,
> Quibus angeli dixere,
> Absit vobis iam timere,
> Natus est rex Gloriae.
>
> Ad quem Magi ambulabant,
> Aurum, thus, myrrham portabant;
> Immolabant haec sincere
> Nato regi gloriae.
>
> Christo regi, Deo nato,
> Per Mariam nobis dato,
> Merito resonet vere
> Laus, honor et gloria.

pastor, -oris (*m*), shepherd
laudavere = laudaverunt
quibus, to whom
absit vobis (+ *infin.*), do
  not . . .
Magus, -i (*m*), wise man
immolo (1), to bring as an offering

Deo nato, born of God,
  born from God
datus, -a, -um, given
merito, deservedly
resonet, may (it) re-echo (the
  subjects are in the last line)
vere, truly

2 *Medieval epitaph from the town of Reading*

quis sum, qualis eram, quid ero, tu mitte rogare.
  nil mea vita refert; ducere disce tuam!

mitte rogare, don't ask
vita, -ae (*f*), life
refert, matters

disce! learn!
tuam (supply **vitam**)

Miranda

MONEY MATTERS

Some derivatives borrowed directly from Latin, without change of form,
can be quite puzzling since they have acquired a new meaning in the
process. Several of these are associated with financial transactions.

The word "creditor" (derived from the Latin verb **credere**, to believe,
trust, entrust) obviously means "a believer" or "a trusting person", but
even in Classical times it had begun to mean "someone who gives you
money or something of monetary value in the belief, well-founded or
otherwise, that he will get it back."

An "auditor" is to us the person who checks the accuracy of a firm's
accounts but must originally have meant "a listener", one who listened
to the explanations offered for the figures presented to him.

It is often difficult to spot a Latin derivative, especially when it undergoes not just a change of meaning but also an alteration in the form of the word. Take, for example, the word "money". The temple of the Roman goddess Juno on Rome's Capitoline Hill, dedicated to **Juno Moneta** (Juno the Adviser), was also used as the place for coining money; and **moneta** thus, by mere chance, came to mean both "mint" and "coined money".

The usual Latin word for "money" (**pecunia**) enshrines an even more basic concept of wealth: it goes back to the Latin word **pecus** "a head of cattle", wealth being measured by the number of cattle one possessed.

Likewise, the word **caput**, as well as meaning "head" in a great many different senses, is also used like **pecus** to mean "a head of cattle". From **caput** further developed the word **capitale**, which is the origin of our words "capital", "chattel" (used of property in general) and "cattle" (property reckoned in livestock).

A pair of words like "chattel" and "cattle" are known as **doublets**, i.e. words of the same derivation, but different in form and meaning. "Mint" and "money" are also doublets.

Aenigma

Clues across

1 mater "celeriter surgite!" inquit. "iam _____ est." (4)

4 quando pueri illam fabulam Corneliae _____? (9)

9 Eucleides _____ et Sextum ad Circum duxit. (2)

11 "in _____ caupona pernoctare nolo" clamat Aurelia. (2)

12 _____ Marci Corneliam in raeda vexabat. (3)

14 "_____!" mussavit Davus. "quam defessus sum!" (4)

15 ego _____ pater in Forum descendemus. (2)

16 _____ mihi cibum, nam valde esurio. (2)

17 quid _____ dicere vis, Sexte? (2)

18 o _____! o mores! (7)

21 omnia _____ diligenter explicavi. (2)

22 ubi nuntius in atrium venit, Corneliam cantantem _____. (8)

24 ubi Cornelii a caupona discesserunt, caupo "_____!" clamavit. (6)

27 quod meam togam diu habebam, novam heri _____. (3)

29 _____ servus Marcum et Sextum docebat. (4)

30 liberi in _____ iter faciunt, tabellarii in cisiis. (6)

32 Sextus pupam _____ Corneliae arripuit. (1,4)

33 "raeda in fossa est" respondit Syrus "sed non mea culpa, nam eam magna arte _____." (3)

34 "quo ambulas, Marce?" "ad Forum _____." (2)

35 caupo quidam hospitem _____ necavit. (4)

Clues down

2 Eucleides in Argiletum ibit et ibi librum _____. (4)

3 multas _____ de urbe Eucleides narravit. (3)

5 multa de hac _____ rogaverunt. (2)

6 duae rotae _____ in fossa manebant. (6)

7 itinera _____ in urbem Cornelia saepe facit. (6)

8 ubi tempus erat discedere, Flaviam complexu _____. (5)

10 "ego dormire volo" _____ Marcus. "noli igitur me excitare!" (6)

12 quod novum librum emere volebam, Argiletum _____. (6)

13 cuius erat illud sepulcrum _____ prope Viam Appiam vidimus? (4)

16 Sextus omnia _____ urbe audire volebat. (2)

17 si bene laborabitis, _____ et Sextum ad ludos cras ducam. (2)

18 numquam antea _____ fabulam audiveram. (5)

19 sonitus muris _____ terruit. (6)

20 quam misera sum! numquam iterum _____ . (6)

23 vide numerum novem supra. (2)

25 "quo is, Eucleides?" "ad tabernam _____." (4)

26 ubi ad tabernam ibo, librum _____ . (4)

28 abhinc tres dies Cornelius ad Curiam _____ . (4)

31 ubi Sextus arborem ascendit, _____ in ramis sedebat. (3)

The solution is on page 96.

Ludi

1 *Latin Scrabble*

Words may be taken only from Books 1 and 2 of *Ecce Romani*, and the player must justify the case or tense ending. Scoring as in ordinary Scrabble. Note that the letter "k" should either be removed from the pile or treated as a "c".

2 *BIS (Latin Snap)*

Make two sets of cards — one white, one yellow. The white cards contain Latin words and the yellow cards the English equivalents. (The Latin words may be straightforward vocabulary items, e.g. nominative singular, infinitive, masculine adjective; or, if a more testing game is required, different persons, tenses, cases, etc., may be introduced.) The white and yellow piles are placed face down on the table.

Play proceeds in a clockwise direction. The players in turn pick a card alternately from the white pile and the yellow pile, and place it face up on to a third pile on the table. When a card of one colour is immediately followed by a card of the other colour which matches the meaning, the player who first shouts "BIS" takes the whole of the third pile. If a wrong call is made, the player misses a turn. The winner is the player who finishes with most cards.

3 *Latin Rummy*

(i) Various sets are possible, e.g.
  (a) the nominative, genitive singular, gender and meaning of a noun;
  (b) principal parts of a verb;
  (c) masculine, feminine, neuter and meaning of an adjective.
It is simpler if the game concentrates on sets of one type, but a mixture of sets is possible, provided there are only four members in each set.

(ii) The aim of the game is to get "out" by building up sets of cards.

(iii) Rules:
  (a) Players draw lots to decide who will be dealer in the first game. The winner of the game becomes the dealer in the next game.
  (b) Each player is dealt ten cards.
  (c) The remaining cards are placed face down in a pile on the table.
  (d) The top card of the pile is turned over to start the "discard" pile.
  (e) Play proceeds in a clockwise direction, starting with the dealer.
  (f) Each player in turn
    1 picks up the top card from one of the piles;
    2 decides whether to lay down (face up) any group of three or

four cards from the same set which are in his/her hand (see Notes 1 and 2 below);

   3 discards one card.

(g) The winner is the player who is able to lay out all the cards in his/her hand, *except one* which is then discarded as the final action of the game.

(h) The other players are penalised by one point for every card still in their hands.

Notes

1 Cards may be laid out only during a player's turn, before discarding.

2 Provided he/she already has a "set" (i.e. at least three cards) on the table, a player may add single cards to part-sets (of any player) already laid out.

4 *The Ben Hur Game*

Make an enlarged photocopy of the Ben Hur game board on p. 60. Colour and decorate it.

Equipment:

  1 dice

  4 coloured counters (red, white, blue and green) representing the different chariot companies (**factiones**): **russati** (reds), **albati** (whites), **veneti** (blues) and **prasini** (greens)

  7 other coloured counters for each of the chariots, representing the wooden eggs (**ova**) which were removed after the completion of each lap

  7 black counters

  34 Incident Cards

Rules:

1 Up to four players (or pairs of players) are allowed.

2 Players draw lots for coloured counters and for the order in which they make their first throw of the dice.

3 Each player throws the dice in turn to decide which track to join at the start of the race, the tracks being numbered from 1 (innermost) to 6 (outermost). (These numbers are ignored in subsequent laps.) If a player throws the same number as a box already occupied, he/she should occupy the box immediately behind that one.

4 In subsequent throws, the number of moves is controlled by the number on the dice and the Incident Card instructions.

5 (a) Incident Cards are shuffled and placed in a pile face down.

  (b) When a player lands on a box marked **?**, he/she picks up an Incident Card and immediately follows the instructions on it.

  (c) If all the cards are used up in the course of a game, they should be reshuffled and again placed in a pile face down.

6 Chariots race in an anti-clockwise direction.

7 Each time a player passes the finishing line one of the eggs (**ova**) of that colour is removed. The number of eggs still showing represents

the number of laps still to be raced. The winner is the chariot which first has the last egg removed.

8 If a player lands on a black square near the turning points (**metae**), the chariot is deemed to have struck the **spina** and must be moved back six squares or, if that square is occupied, to the next available box behind that. At the same time, the player collects a black counter. If 2 black counters are collected, the player has crashed completely and is out of the race.

9 In the course of a move a chariot may not enter or pass through a square occupied by another chariot. To avoid a collision the chariot may (a) stop behind the other chariot, or (b) use up the remaining moves by moving one square to the right, or two squares to the right and then forward.

10 If a player lands in a box from which an arrow emerges, the move to the next box is made immediately and before the next player throws the dice. If the arrow leads to a box which is already occupied, the player has swerved into another chariot and must withdraw 2 boxes behind the chariot.

11 If the player has to move to the right or left under penalty and reaches the outer wall or the **spina** before using up the penalty moves, the remaining moves shall be backwards in the outside or inside track.

12 If a player has to move backwards under penalty and lands on a box already occupied, he/she must keep moving farther back in the same track until an empty box is reached.

Contents of Incident Cards
Make two cards for each of the following:

(a) You have lost control of your horses. Move back 3 squares.

(b) Keep your eyes on the race and not on your admirers in the crowd. Move 2 squares to the right.

(c) Well done! You have seen an opening. Move forward 3 squares.

(d) Wreckage ahead! Move 2 tracks to left or right before moving on.

(e) One of your horses has gone lame. Lose a turn.

(f) A chariot has swerved in front of you. Move 2 spaces to the left.

(g) Swerve 2 boxes to right or you will hit one of the slaves clearing the track.

(h) Swerve 2 boxes to left or you will hit one of the slaves clearing the track.

(i) Force your way through. If a chariot is in your way, move it one square to the right.

(j) Loose wheel! Move 3 boxes to the right.

(k) Your whip has become entangled with another driver's. Go back 3 spaces.

(l) Other drivers' whips have become entangled. All those in tracks numbered lower than yours must move back 3 spaces.

(m) There is an opening on your right. Move to the next Incident Card box in the track immediately to the right of your present track and follow the instructions on the Card.

(n) You have been startled by a great roar from the crowd and momentarily lose control of the horses. Move three squares to the right.

(o) The free-running horse on the right side of your team has swung away from the pair harnessed in the middle. Move 2 boxes to the right.

(p) One of your reins has snapped. Miss a turn.

(q) Your superior skill with the whip makes your horses surge forward. Go forward four spaces. If another chariot is in your way, move it one square to the right.

For those interested in wargaming, a more sophisticated "Circus Maximus" game may be bought from T.M. Games, Chart House, Station Road, East Preston, Littlehampton, West Sussex BN16 3AG.

Footnote
Although the Ben Hur game is the copyright of the Scottish Classics Group, teachers may enlarge the board by photocopying it, and they may also reproduce the contents of the Incident Cards for use in the classroom.

The chariot race from the film *Ben Hur.*

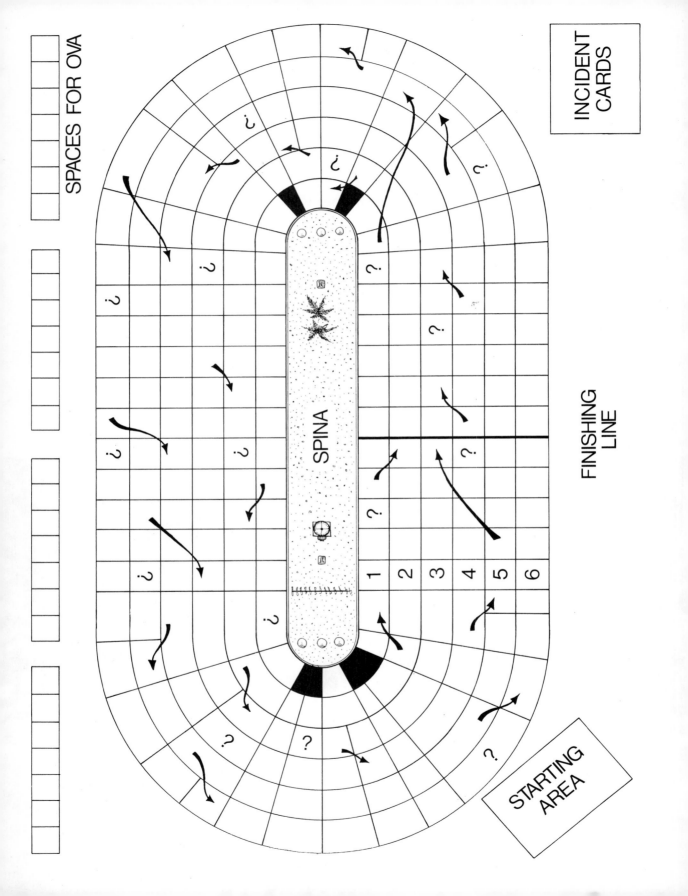

Fabricanda

Toga

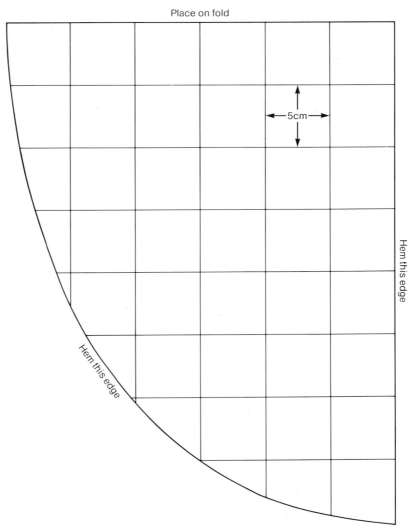

Place on fold

5cm

Hem this edge

Hem this edge

This pattern fits a doll 28.5 cm tall.
Make a full-scale pattern in newspaper, tissue paper, greaseproof paper or graph paper.

Material required:
A piece of white or off-white flannelette, Viyella or muslin 90 × 35 cm

Instructions:
1 Fold the material in half.
2 Place the pattern with the edge on the fold as shown on the pattern.
3 Cut out one piece, allowing 1.5 cm all round for a hem.

How to put on the toga praetexta

The toga you have made will fit a doll of the size stated. You could make one to fit you from an old sheet or curtain. This is how you put it on:

1. Ask someone to help you, just as Roman senators would normally have done.
2. Drape the toga over your left shoulder (Fig. 2) in such a way that
   (i) point C (roughly a third of the way along the straight purple edge) is touching the left side of your neck,
   (ii) the curved side hangs down your left arm,
   (iii) point A is on the floor in front of you, and
   (iv) the rest of the toga is hanging down behind.
3. With your right hand, pull across your back and under your right arm the part that is hanging down behind.
4. Now fold over the part mentioned in step 3 in such a way as to make a straight edge through point D (see Fig. 1), roughly in the proportions 2:1 so that one third hangs down to the level of E, and the two-thirds fall to F (Fig. 3).
5. Throw the end of the folded cloth (see step 4) over your left shoulder so that point B falls to the floor behind you (Fig. 4).
6. Step 4 should produce a double **sinus** (see footnote): the first (the straight edge made at D when the cloth is folded over) runs from under the right arm across the chest and over the left shoulder, and looks like a shoulder-belt, although it should not be tight against the chest like a belt; the second (formed by the straight purple edge which has been doubled over) runs from about the level of the right knee up over the left shoulder (i.e. the thick line beginning at E in Fig. 3).
7. Adjust the toga on your shoulder so that point B almost touches the floor behind you (Fig. 4). This can be done by increasing or decreasing the folds mentioned in step 6.

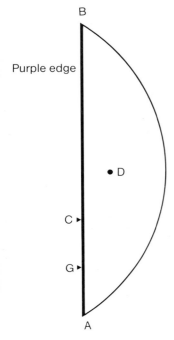

Purple edge

Fig. 1

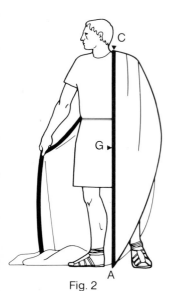

Fig. 2

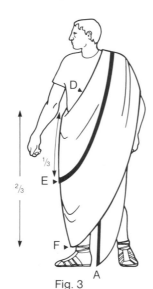

Fig. 3

Fig. 4

Fig. 5

8 Finally, to avoid point A trailing on the ground and possibly tripping you,
   (a) put your hand inside the toga behind D,
   (b) take hold of point G, roughly at waist level (Fig. 2),
   (c) pull G up and out from behind the straight edge passing through D,
   (d) let G hang over in a fold (**sinus**) (Fig. 5) in front of the straight edge which passes through D.

Footnote: The Latin word **sinus** describes anything shaped like a curve, e.g. bay, gulf, hollow, valley, bosom, lap, fold in cloth.

Tunica

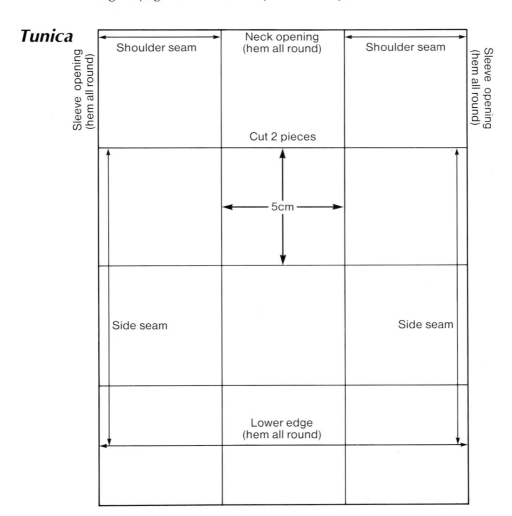

This will fit a doll 28.5 cm tall.

Make a full-scale pattern. Try it on the doll and reduce the width so that the shoulder seam does not come down the arm too far.

Cut out two pieces of material and sew them together as instructed.

Currus

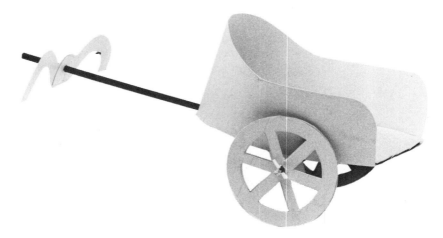

Materials required:

card

3mm dowelling or Jiffy-
  sticks (obtained from
  garden centre)

corrugated cardboard

glue

small pieces of split matchstick
  (for axle pins)

Note:
- (a) All measurements are in millimetres.
- (b) The plans are for a model made from card. If wood is used, no tabs are necessary; and either the shaft would have to be glued under the floor of the chariot or a recess cut for it in the floor.
- (c) *Cut* continuous lines; *fold* broken lines. It is advisable to *score* broken lines with the point of scissors before folding.
- (d) Cut away shaded areas (D).

Instructions:
1. Using the measurements shown, copy the pattern pieces and cut out as instructed.
2. Glue the card floors (F) above and below the corrugated cardboard floor (G). This creates thickness for gluing in the shaft.
3. In the side wall (H), cut the hole (L) for the shaft above the centre (E) tab and also the holes (K) for the axle.
4. Fix the side wall (H) to the floor by gluing the tabs (E) under the floor.
5. From 3mm dowelling or a Jiffystick make a shaft 100 mm long. Glue the shaft in the groove marked (C).
6. Cut out 4 wheels from card and glue two together to make 2 stronger wheels.
7. From dowelling or a Jiffystick make an axle 55 mm long. Make a hole for an axle pin (a small piece of split matchstick) at either end. Put the first wheel on the axle and insert a pin through the hole.
8. Put the axle through the holes (K) at the foot of the side wall.
9. Put on the second wheel and insert the axle pin.
10. Put the yoke on the end of the shaft.

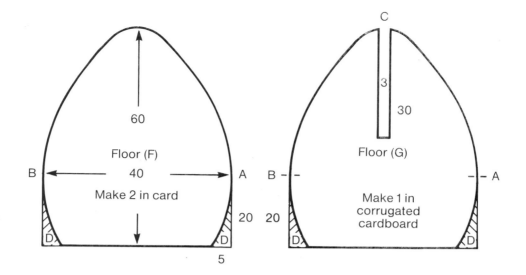

Floor (F)

60

B ← 40 → A

Make 2 in card

20   20

D   D

5

Floor (G)

C

3

30

B –   – A

Make 1 in
corrugated
cardboard

D   D

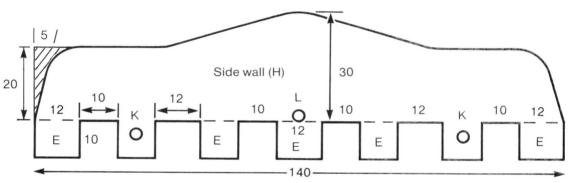

Side wall (H)

5 /

20

30

12

10

K

12

10

L

12

E

10

E

10

E

10

E

12

K

10

12

E

E

140

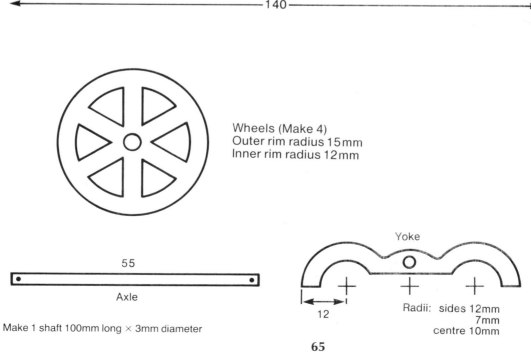

Wheels (Make 4)
Outer rim radius 15mm
Inner rim radius 12mm

55

Axle

Make 1 shaft 100mm long × 3mm diameter

Yoke

12

Radii: sides 12mm
7mm
centre 10mm

Cisium

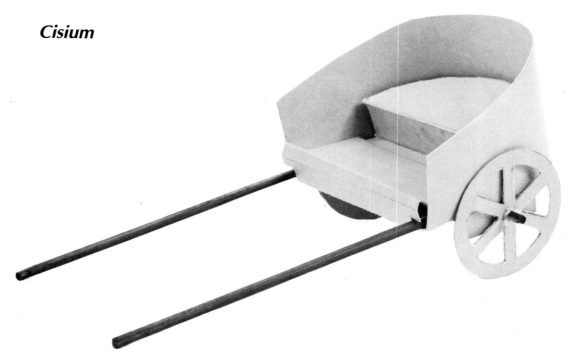

Materials:

card	3mm dowelling or Jiffysticks
corrugated cardboard	(obtainable from garden centre)
glue	small pieces of split matchstick
	(for axle pins)

Note:

All measurements are in millimetres.

Cut continuous lines; *fold* broken lines; *score* broken lines with point of scissors before folding.

Instructions:

1. Using the measurements shown, cut out the various pieces that make up the **cisium**.
2. Glue the corrugated cardboard shape (A) to one of the shapes marked (B).
3. Glue the shafts (made from dowelling or Jiffysticks) into the spaces marked (C).
4. To cover the shafts, glue the second shape marked (B) on top of the corrugated cardboard part (A).
5. Make two axle holes (E) in the side-wall (D).
6. Glue the side-wall (D) into position by gluing the tabs under the floor.
7. Glue the seat (F) into position.
8. Glue the footboard (G) in position in front of the seat.
9. Glue two wheels together, for added strength, and make holes for the axle.
10. Insert the axle, put a wheel on each end and insert an axle pin (a small piece of split matchstick) through the hole at the end of the axle.

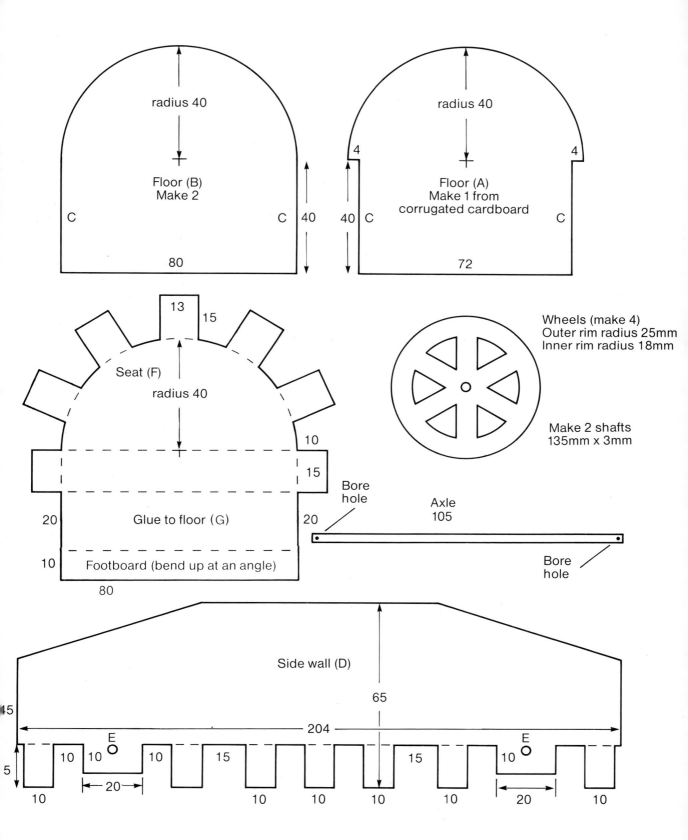

radius 40

Floor (B)
Make 2

C   C   40

80

radius 40

Floor (A)
Make 1 from
corrugated cardboard

4   4

40   C   C

72

13   15

Seat (F)

radius 40

10

15

20   Glue to floor (G)   20

10   Footboard (bend up at an angle)

80

Wheels (make 4)
Outer rim radius 25mm
Inner rim radius 18mm

Make 2 shafts
135mm x 3mm

Bore
hole

Axle
105

Bore
hole

Side wall (D)

65

45

204

E   E

10   10   10   15   15   10

5

10   20   10   10   10   10   20   10

Roman litter
(Lectica)

Materials:

card	cloth (for curtains)
glue	fine wire (for curtain rails)
3mm dowelling or Jiffysticks	scraps of material (for mattress and pillow)

Note:
(a) All measurements are in millimetres.
(b) The plans are for models made from card. If wood is used, no tabs are necessary.
(c) *Cut* continuous lines; *fold* broken lines; *score* broken lines with point of scissors before folding.
(d) Use compasses to draw the arches. The centre point is marked with a cross.

Instructions:
Using the measurements shown, cut out the pieces that make up the litter.

The main body
1 Make all folds first.
2 Make the four holes for the shafts in the end-sections (A) and (B) and cut the holes (D) for the legs.
3 Glue the end pillars to the end-sections (A) and (B).
4 Glue the side to the tabs marked (C).

The curtains
Cut pieces of cloth to fit and either glue them in position or, if you wish to be able to open and close them, use fine wire as curtain rails.

When using wire, bore small holes near the top ends of the legs. Push the wire through the first hole; put on the first curtain; insert the wire through the next hole, and so on.

The legs

Make these from 3mm dowelling or Jiffysticks. Glue them inside the corner pillars of the main body of the litter, through the holes marked (D).

The roof

1 Glue the tabs (E) on the *outside* of the corner pillars.
2 Glue the tabs (F) on the *outside* of the end walls.
3 To cover the tabs at the ends, make two curved sections (G). Add some sort of decoration to the top. Glue these in position.

Finally, insert the shafts (made from dowelling or Jiffysticks) and place in the litter a small mattress with raised pillow.

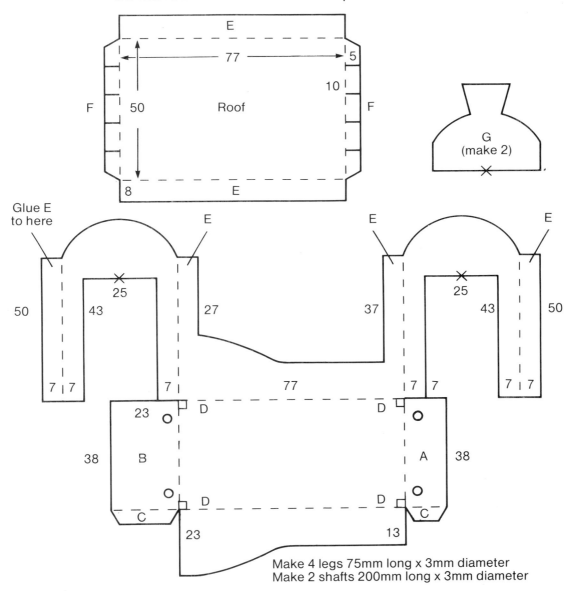

Make 4 legs 75mm long x 3mm diameter
Make 2 shafts 200mm long x 3mm diameter

Raeda

Materials:

card

corrugated cardboard

glue

3mm dowelling or Jiffysticks

small piece of material (for curtains)

thread

small pieces of split matchstick
(for axle pins)

Note:
- (a) All measurements are in millimetres.
- (b) The plans are for a model made from card. If wood is used, no tabs are necessary.
- (c) *Cut* continuous lines; *fold* broken lines; *score* broken lines with point of scissors before folding.
- (d) Use compasses to draw the curved roof. The centre point is marked with a cross.

Instructions:

1 Following the measurements shown, cut out the pieces of the raeda.

2 *The main body*
- (a) Make all folds first.
- (b) Cut out windows and, if desired, cut round three sides of the door. Fold back the shaded areas of the windows and glue them down, for added strength.
- (c) Cut the holes for the shafts at the end that has no window.
- (d) Glue tabs (B) to the sides, to make a roofless "box".
- (e) Insert and glue the axle tabs (E) through slits (D).
- (f) Insert the corrugated cardboard floor, making sure that the slits for the shafts are at the end with no window.
- (g) Make shafts from 3mm dowelling or Jiffysticks. Glue them into the slits marked (F).
- (h) Insert the passenger seats.

3 Tie the bottoms of the curtains together with thread and glue them to the top of the body frame. It may also be necessary to glue the bottoms of the curtains to the side wall.

4 Glue the roof on top of tabs (A) and on the outside of the walls (C).

5 Glue the driver's seat on the end-wall above the shafts. The 10 mm part is the seat top; and half of the last 20 mm is the extended platform for the driver's feet.

6 *The wheels*
   (a) Glue the wheels together in pairs (for added strength).
   (b) Push one wheel on to the axle and insert an axle pin (a small piece
       of split matchstick) through the hole at the end of the axle.
   (c) Put the axle through the tabs (E).
   (d) Put on the second wheel and insert the axle pin.
   (e) Repeat for the other two wheels.

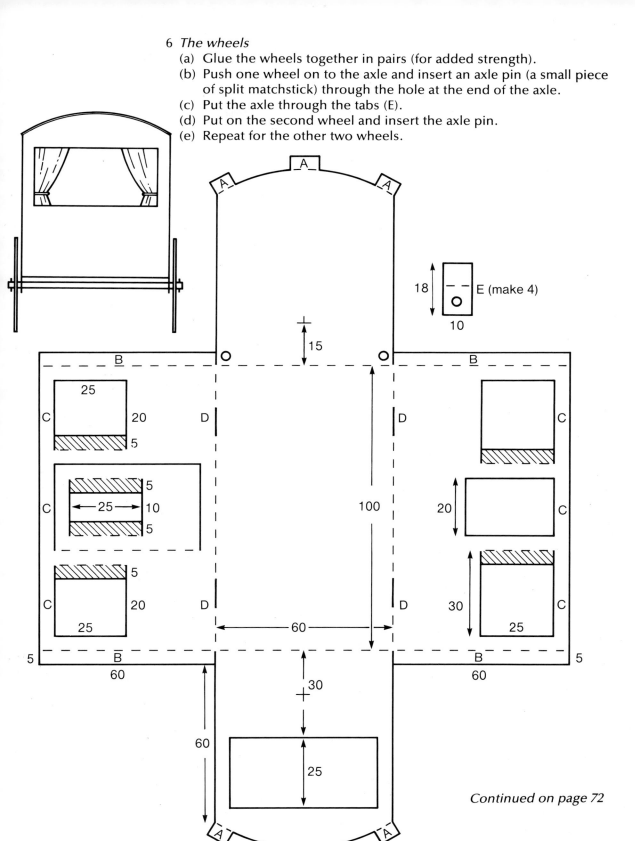

E (make 4)
18
10

A
A
A

B
B
C
25
20
5
C
C
5
25 10
5
D
D
100
D
D
20
C
30
25
C
15
C
25
20
C
25
60
5
B
B
5
60
60
30
60
25

Continued on page 72

A
A
A 5

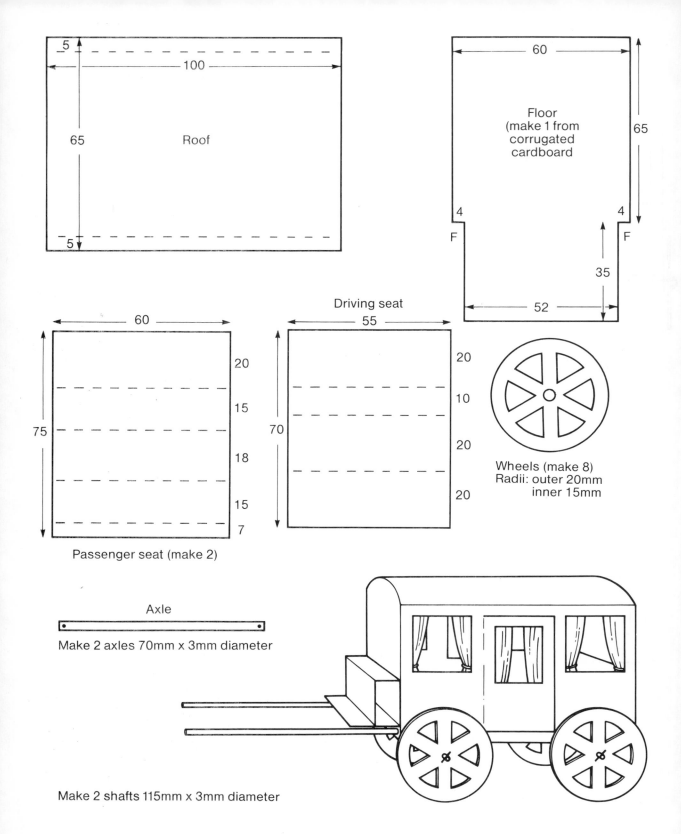

5

100

65

Roof

5

60

Floor
(make 1 from
corrugated
cardboard

65

4

F

4

F

35

52

60

Driving seat

55

20

20

15

10

75

18

70

20

15

20

7

Passenger seat (make 2)

Wheels (make 8)
Radii: outer 20mm
inner 15mm

Axle

Make 2 axles 70mm x 3mm diameter

Make 2 shafts 115mm x 3mm diameter

Roman Gate
(Porta)

Materials:

card   glue

stiff paper   piece of strong cardboard

Note:

(a) All measurements are in millimetres.

(b) The plans are for a model made from card. Paper is strong enough for the under side of the arches.

(c) *Cut* continuous lines; *fold* broken lines; *score* broken lines with the point of scissors before folding.

(d) If wood is used, no tabs are necessary.

(e) Use compasses to draw the tops of the arches. The centre point for using compasses is marked with a cross.

(f) The windows (K) and (L) may be cut out or painted.

Instructions:

1 Using the measurements shown, draw the pattern pieces and cut them out.

2 Make all the necessary folds.

3 Glue the main "box" (gateway section) together as follows;

    (a) Glue the tab marked (A) to the side marked (A).

    (b) Glue the 5 tabs marked (B) to the 5 tabs marked (C).

    (c) Glue the 2 tabs marked (D) to the end tabs (B/C).

    (d) Glue the tab marked (H) behind the parapet (i.e. on the inside of the "box"), and the tabs marked (J) over the top of the sides marked (S), i.e. glue them on the outside of the "box".

4 Fix the paper inside the arches as follows:

    (a) Glue (G) to the end base-section (B/C).

    (b) Push the 34 mm length into the area of the small arch, but do not glue it yet.

    (c) Glue (F) to the base-section (B/C) between the large and small arches.

    (d) Push the 70 mm length into the area of the large arch, but do not glue it yet. The 4 mm slits will splay at the top of the arches.

    (e) Glue (E) to the base-section (B/C) between the two large arches.

    (f) Glue the tabs round the front and back of the arch-pillars (upright parts first) and then the tabs at the top of the arches.

    (g) Repeat the operation for the other two arches.

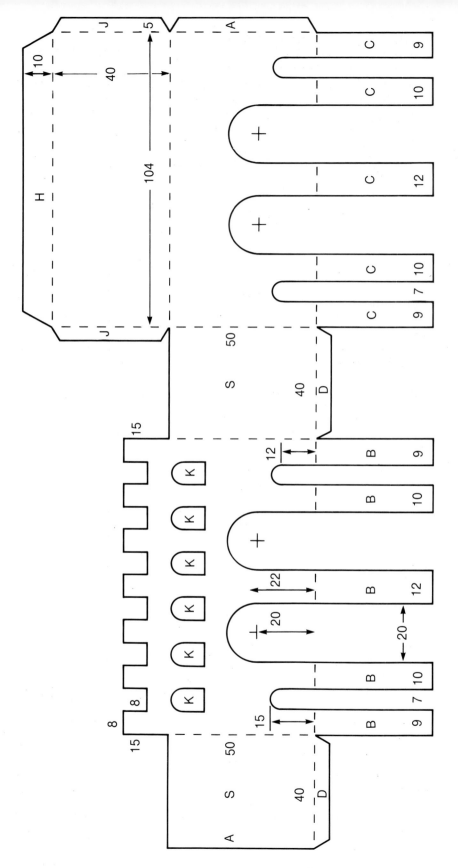

Gateway section

5 Construct each tower as follows:
   (a) Bend the curved wall round (P) and glue tabs (M) and (N) in
        position on the inside of the tower.
   (b) Glue the base (Q) in position by means of the tabs marked (R),
        gluing these on the outside of the base.
6 Finally, glue the completed model to a cardboard base-stand. First,
   glue the "box" (gateway section) to the centre of the stand and then,
   on each side of the gateway, glue on the towers.

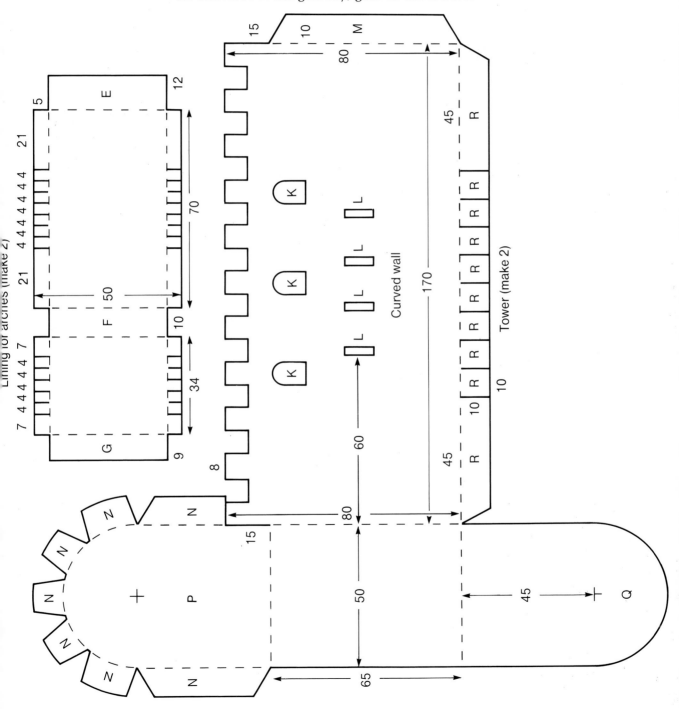

Tables

Section A: Nouns

		Group 1	Group 2			Group 3		Group 4	Group 5
Sing.	Nom.	puella	servus	puer	baculum	vox	civis	nomen	manus	dies
	Acc.	puellam	servum	puerum	baculum	vocem	civem	nomen	manum	diem
	Gen.	puellae	servi	pueri	baculi	vocis	civis	nominis	manus	diei
	Dat.	puellae	servo	puero	baculo	voci	civi	nomini	manui	diei
	Abl.	puella	servo	puero	baculo	voce	cive	nomine	manu	die
Plur.	Nom.	puellae	servi	pueri	bacula	voces	cives	nomina	manus	dies
	Acc.	puellas	servos	pueros	bacula	voces	cives	nomina	manus	dies
	Gen.	puellarum	servorum	puerorum	baculorum	vocum	civium	nominum	manuum	dierum
	Dat.	puellis	servis	pueris	baculis	vocibus	civibus	nominibus	manibus	diebus
	Abl.	puellis	servis	pueris	baculis	vocibus	civibus	nominibus	manibus	diebus

1 *Vocative Case.* This case is used when someone or something is addressed by name. It is only in the singular of Group 2 nouns ending in **-us** that it has a different ending from the nominative case, e.g. **Sexte, Marce, Corneli, Gai, amice.**

2 In Group 3 nouns, there is no standard form for the nominative singular (e.g. **mater, vestis, urbs,** etc.); and there are two forms of the genitive plural (**-um** and **-ium**).

3 The *stem* of a noun is that part which remains when the genitive singular ending is removed, e.g. **puella**, genitive singular **puellae,** stem **puell-; vox, vocis,** stem **voc-; nomen, nominis,** stem **nomin-.**

4 **domus** usually has the same endings as **manus.** Common exceptions are ablative singular (**domo**) and the special form **domi,** *at home.*

5 *Gender:*
  (a) Group 1 nouns are all feminine except for those which are men's names, jobs that men did, or the names of certain rivers, e.g. **Caligula, -ae** (*m*): **agricola, -ae** (*m*), *farmer;* **Matrona, -ae** (*m*), *Marne.*

  (b) Group 2 nouns ending in **-us** or **-er** are nearly all masculine, but names of cities, islands and trees are feminine, e.g. **Corinthus, -i** (*f*), *Corinth;* **laurus, -i** (*f*), *bay-tree.* Group 2 nouns ending in **-um** are neuter.

  (c) Most nouns in Group 3 are either masculine or feminine, but nearly all nouns of the following types are neuter:
    ending in **-en, -inis** : e.g. **nomen, nominis** (*n*)
    ending in **-us, -oris** : e.g. **corpus, corporis** (*n*)
    ending in **-us, -eris** : e.g. **onus, oneris** (*n*)

  (d) Group 4 nouns ending in **-us** are all mostly masculine, but two common exceptions are **manus, -us** (*f*) and **domus, -us** (*f*).

  (e) Group 5 nouns are all feminine except **dies, diei** (*m*) and **meridies, -ei** (*m*). When **dies** refers to a fixed day it is feminine, e.g. **die constituta,** *on the appointed day.*

Section B: Adjectives

		Group 1/2			Group 3			
		Masc.	Fem.	Neut.	Masc./Fem.	Neut.	Masc./Fem.	Neut.
Sing.	Nom.	magnus	magna	magnum	omnis	omne	ingens	ingens
	Acc.	magnum	magnam	magnum	omnem	omne	ingentem	ingens
	Gen.	magni	magnae	magni	omnis	omnis	ingentis	ingentis
	Dat.	magno	magnae	magno	omni	omni	ingenti	ingenti
	Abl.	magno	magna	magno	omni	omni	ingenti	ingenti
Plur.	Nom.	magni	magnae	magna	omnes	omnia	ingentes	ingentia
	Acc.	magnos	magnas	magna	omnes	omnia	ingentes	ingentia
	Gen.	magnorum	magnarum	magnorum	omnium	omnium	ingentium	ingentium
	Dat.	magnis	magnis	magnis	omnibus	omnibus	ingentibus	ingentibus
	Abl.	magnis	magnis	magnis	omnibus	omnibus	ingentibus	ingentibus

1 In general, nouns and adjectives of the same group have the same case endings. Thus,

magnus has the same endings as **servus**

magna has the same endings as **puella**

magnum has the same endings as **baculum**.

However, in Group 3, whereas most nouns have their ablative singular ending in -e, most adjectives have their ablative singular ending in -i. Exceptions are **dives** (*rich*), **pauper, -eris** (*poor*), **vetus, -eris** (*old*) and comparative adjectives which have their ablative singular ending in -e.

2 Some adjectives of Group 1/2 end in -er in the nominative singular masculine, e.g.

noster, nostra, nostrum

miser, misera, miserum.

The endings of the other cases are the same as for **magnus, -a, -um**.

3 There is no standard form for the nominative singular endings of Group 3 adjectives.

Section C: Personal Pronouns and Possessive Adjectives

Personal Pronouns

		1st Person	2nd Person
Sing.	Nom.	ego	tu
	Acc.	me	te
	Gen.	mei	tui
	Dat.	mihi	tibi
	Abl.	me	te
Plur.	Nom.	nos	vos
	Acc.	nos	vos
	Gen.	nostrum	vestrum
	Dat.	nobis	vobis
	Abl.	nobis	vobis

Possessive Adjectives

	1st Person	2nd Person
	meus, -a, -um, *my*	tuus, -a, -um, *your*
	noster, -tra, -trum, *our*	vester, -tra, -trum, *your*

Possessive Adjective:

Acc.	se
Gen.	sui
Dat.	sibi
Abl.	se

Possessive Adjective:
suus, -a, -um *his, her, its, their*

Notes:

1 For the 3rd person, see the Notes on Demonstrative Adjectives on page 80.

2 The Personal Pronouns are also used as Reflexive Pronouns in the 1st and 2nd persons, e.g. **me servavi**, *I saved* **myself**. **nos** liberavimus, *We set* **ourselves** *free.*

3 A special Reflexive Pronoun is used in the 3rd person (singular and plural) meaning *himself, herself, itself, themselves:*

4 The preposition **cum** is used *after* Personal and Reflexive Pronouns, e.g. **mecum**, *with me;* **nobiscum**, *with us;* **secum**, *with himself.*

78

Section D: Interrogative, Relative and Indefinite Pronouns

		Interrogative Pronoun (who? what?)			Relative Pronoun (who, which, that)			Indefinite Pronoun (a certain)		
		Masc.	Fem.	Neut.	Masc.	Fem.	Neut.	Masc.	Fem.	Neut.
Sing.	Nom.	quis?	quis?	quid?	qui	quae	quod	quidam	quaedam	quoddam
	Acc.	quem?	quem?	quid?	quem	quam	quod	quendam	quandam	quoddam
	Gen.	cuius?	cuius?	cuius?	cuius	cuius	cuius	cuiusdam	cuiusdam	cuiusdam
	Dat.	cui?	cui?	cui?	cui	cui	cui	cuidam	cuidam	cuidam
	Abl.	quo?	qua?	quo?	quo	qua	quo	quodam	quadam	quodam
Plur.	Nom.	qui?	quae?	quae?	qui	quae	quae	quidam	quaedam	quaedam
	Acc.	quos?	quas?	quae?	quos	quas	quae	quosdam	quasdam	quaedam
	Gen.	quorum?	quarum?	quorum?	quorum	quarum	quorum	quorundam	quarundam	quorundam
	Dat.	quibus?	quibus?	quibus?	quibus	quibus	quibus	quibusdam	quibusdam	quibusdam
	Abl.	quibus?	quibus?	quibus?	quibus	quibus	quibus	quibusdam	quibusdam	quibusdam

Notes:

1 The Relative and Interrogative Pronouns have the same forms, except in the nominative and accusative singular.

2 The Interrogative Adjective has the same forms as the Relative Pronoun, e.g. **quod** templum visitavisti? *Which temple did you visit?*

3 **quidam, quaedam, quoddam** (*a certain*) is a compound of the Relative Pronoun and the ending **-dam.** It has the same forms as the Relative Pronoun, except that **-m-** changes to **-n-** before **-d.** (Cf. **idem.**) **quidam** is used both as a pronoun and as an adjective, e.g. **quidam** advenit. **A certain man** *has arrived.* homines **quosdam** vidimus. *We saw* **some men**.

Section E: Demonstrative Adjectives

		Masc.	Fem.	Neut.	Masc.	Fem.	Neut.	Masc.	Fem.	Neut.
Sing.	Nom.	hic	haec	hoc	ille	illa	illud	is	ea	id
	Acc.	hunc	hanc	hoc	illum	illam	illud	eum	eam	id
	Gen.	huius	huius	huius	illius	illius	illius	eius	eius	eius
	Dat.	huic	huic	huic	illi	illi	illi	ei	ei	ei
	Abl.	hoc	hac	hoc	illo	illa	illo	eo	ea	eo
Plur.	Nom.	hi	hae	haec	illi	illae	illa	ei	eae	ea
	Acc.	hos	has	haec	illos	illas	illa	eos	eas	ea
	Gen.	horum	harum	horum	illorum	illarum	illorum	eorum	earum	eorum
	Dat.	his	his	his	illis	illis	illis	eis	eis	eis
	Abl.	his	his	his	illis	illis	illis	eis	eis	eis

Notes:

1 **eam** puellam vidimus. *We saw* **that** *girl.*
   haec mulier cum **eis** pueris ambulabat. **This** *woman was walking with* **those** *boys.*
   ille senator risit. **That** *senator laughed.*

2 The above Demonstrative Adjectives are also used as 3rd person
   pronouns,
   e.g. **eam** vidimus. *We saw* **her.**
   haec cum **eis** ambulabat. **She** *was walking with* **them.**
   ille risit. **He** *laughed.*

3 The genitive forms are used to express *his, her, its, their,*
   e.g. ego sum dominus **eius.** *I am* **his** *master.*
   ad villam **eorum** venit. *He came to* **their** *villa.*
   (See also Note 3 on page 78.)

		Masc.	Fem.	Neut.	Masc.	Fem.	Neut.
Sing.	Nom.	idem	eadem	idem	ipse	ipsa	ipsum
	Acc.	eundem	eandem	idem	ipsum	ipsam	ipsum
	Gen.	eiusdem	eiusdem	eiusdem	ipsius	ipsius	ipsius
	Dat.	eidem	eidem	eidem	ipsi	ipsi	ipsi
	Abl.	eodem	eadem	eodem	ipso	ipsa	ipso
Plur.	Nom.	eidem	eaedem	eadem	ipsi	ipsae	ipsa
	Acc.	eosdem	easdem	eadem	ipsos	ipsas	ipsa
	Gen.	eorundem	earundem	eorundem	ipsorum	ipsarum	ipsorum
	Dat.	eisdem	eisdem	eisdem	ipsis	ipsis	ipsis
	Abl.	eisdem	eisdem	eisdem	ipsis	ipsis	ipsis

Notes:

1 **idem, eadem, idem,** *the same,* has the same forms as **is, ea, id** with the addition of
   -dem. Note that **-m-** is changed to **-n-** in the accusative singular (masc. and fem.)
   and in the genitive plural; and the nominative and accusative singular neuter is **idem.**

2 **ipse, ipsa, ipsum** is used to give emphasis to a noun or pronoun, e.g.
   ego **ipse** veni. *I* **myself** *came.*
   Caesarem **ipsum** vidimus. *We saw Caesar* **himself.**   **ipse** venit. *He* **himself** *came.*
   aedificia **ipsa** vidimus. *We saw the* **actual** *buildings.*
   the **very** *buildings.*
   the buildings **themselves.**

Section F: Prepositions

1 Prepositions followed by the *accusative* case:

ad, to, towards, at, near	**ad** eam currit. **ad** Portam Capenam exspectabat. **ad** raedam stabat.	*He runs* **towards** *her.* *He was waiting* **at** *the Porta Capena.* *She was standing* **near** *the coach.*
ante, before, in front of	**ante** villam ambulant.	*They are walking* **in front of** *the house.*
circum, round	**circum** arborem currunt.	*They are running* **round** *the tree.*
extra, outside	**extra** urbem ibimus.	*We shall go* **outside** *the city.*
inter, between, among	**inter** villam et agros est hortus.	*There is a garden* **between** *the house and the fields.*
intra, inside	sunt multae viae **intra** urbem.	*There are many streets* **inside** *the city.*
per, along, through	**per** Viam Appiam iter faciebant. **per** agros celeriter currebant.	*They were journeying* **along** *the Via Appia.* *They ran swiftly* **through** *the fields.*
post, after	**post** cenam cubitum iverunt.	*They went to bed* **after** *dinner.*
praeter, past, beyond	**praeter** sepulcrum iter faciunt.	*They journey* **past** *the tomb.*
prope, near	servi **prope** viam quiescunt.	*The slaves are resting* **near** *the road.*
supra, above	pontem **supra** Portam video.	*I see a bridge* **above** *the Gate.*
trans, across	**trans** aream venit Eucleides.	*Eucleides comes* **across** *the yard.*

2 Prepositions followed by the *ablative* case:

a, ab, by, from	**ab** urbe venerunt.	*They came* **from** *the city.*
cum, with	Cornelia **cum** amica ambulabat.	*Cornelia was walking* **with** *her friend.*
de, concerning, about, down	miles fabulam **de** caupone narrat. **de** arbore descendit.	*The soldier tells a story* **about** *an innkeeper.* *He climbed* **down from** *the tree.*
e, ex, out of, from	servi **ex** area currunt.	*The slaves run* **out of** *the yard.*
pro, in front of	**pro** patre stabat.	*He was standing* **in front of** *his father.*
sine, without	est periculosum **sine** custode exire.	*It is dangerous to go out* **without** *a guard.*
sub, under	**sub** arboribus quiescebant.	*They were resting* **under** *the trees.*

3 The preposition **in** is used with the *accusative* and the *ablative*.

in (+ *accus.*), into, to **in** (+ *abl.*), in, on	Marcus **in** villam statim currit. **in** pictura est puella. **in** lecto iacet.	*Marcus runs immediately* **into** *the house.* **In** *the picture is a girl.* *He is lying* **on** *the bed.*

Section G: Verbs

(a) *Person Endings*

	Active	
Person	All tenses except Perfect	Perfect
1 I 2 you 3 he, she, it	-o, -m -s -t	-i -isti -it
1 we 2 you 3 they	-mus -tis -nt	-imus -istis -erunt

(b) *Principal Parts*

When we refer to Latin verbs, we normally give four principal parts and their meaning, e.g.

	Present Indicative	Present Infinitive	Perfect Indicative	Supine	Meaning
Group 1 Group 2 Group 3 Group 4	porto habeo mitto facio audio	portare (1) habere (2) mittere (3) facere (3) audire (4)	portavi habui misi feci audivi	portatum habitum missum factum auditum	*to carry* *to have* *to send* *to make, do* *to hear*

Most verbs in Groups 1, 2 and 4 follow the above patterns. There is no standard form for verbs in Group 3. This section will help you if you know which verb you are dealing with but are in some doubt about the form which is used.

All parts of a verb can be identified from the four principal parts. The following table of the verb **portare** illustrates the forms you have met so far:

Principal Parts	porto, portare Present stem: **porta-**			portavi Perfect stem: **portav-**		
Indicative	Present	**porto**	I carry I am carrying	Perfect	**portavi**	I carried I have carried I did carry
	Imperfect	**portabam**	I carried I was carrying I used to carry I kept on carrying I began to carry	Pluperfect	**portaveram**	I had carried
	Future	**portabo**	I shall carry I will carry			
Infinitive	Present	**portare**	to carry			
Imperative		**porta** **portate**	carry!			
Participle	Present	**portans**	carrying			

Parts of the verb which are formed from the Supine will be met in Book 3 of *Ecce Romani*.

Regular Verbs

Group	Present	Imperfect	Future
1 **portare**	porto portas portat portamus portatis portant	portabam portabas portabat portabamus portabatis portabant	portabo portabis portabit portabimus portabitis portabunt
2 **habere**	habeo habes habet habemus habetis habent	habebam habebas habebat habebamus habebatis habebant	habebo habebis habebit habebimus habebitis habebunt
3 **mittere**	mitto mittis mittit mittimus mittitis mittunt	mittebam mittebas mittebat mittebamus mittebatis mittebant	mittam mittes mittet mittemus mittetis mittent
facere	facio facis facit facimus facitis faciunt	faciebam faciebas faciebat faciebamus faciebatis faciebant	faciam facies faciet faciemus facietis facient
4 **audire**	audio audis audit audimus auditis audiunt	audiebam audiebas audiebat audiebamus audiebatis audiebant	audiam audies audiet audiemus audietis audient

Perfect	Pluperfect
portavi portavisti portavit portavimus portavistis portaverunt	portaveram portaveras portaverat portaveramus portaveratis portaverant
habui habuisti habuit habuimus habuistis habuerunt	habueram habueras habuerat habueramus habueratis habuerant
misi misisti misit misimus misistis miserunt	miseram miseras miserat miseramus miseratis miserant
feci fecisti fecit fecimus fecistis fecerunt	feceram feceras fecerat feceramus feceratis fecerant
audivi audivisti audivit audivimus audivistis audiverunt	audiveram audiveras audiverat audiveramus audiveratis audiverant

Irregular Verbs

Infinitive	Present	Imperfect	Future	Perfect	Pluperfect
esse	sum es est sumus estis sunt	eram eras erat eramus eratis erant	ero eris erit erimus eritis erunt	fui fuisti fuit fuimus fuistis fuerunt	fueram fueras fuerat fueramus fueratis fuerant
posse	possum potes potest possumus potestis possunt	poteram poteras poterat poteramus poteratis poterant	potero poteris poterit poterimus poteritis poterunt	potui potuisti potuit potuimus potuistis potuerunt	potueram potueras potuerat potueramus potueratis potuerant
ire	eo is it imus itis eunt	ibam ibas ibat ibamus ibatis ibant	ibo ibis ibit ibimus ibitis ibunt	ivi ivisti ivit ivimus ivistis iverunt	iveram iveras iverat iveramus iveratis iverant
velle	volo vis vult volumus vultis volunt	volebam volebas volebat volebamus volebatis volebant	volam voles volet volemus voletis volent	volui voluisti voluit voluimus voluistis voluerunt	volueram volueras voluerat volueramus volueratis voluerant
nolle	nolo nonvis nonvult nolumus nonvultis nolunt	nolebam nolebas nolebat nolebamus nolebatis nolebant	nolam noles nolet nolemus noletis nolent	nolui noluisti noluit noluimus noluistis noluerunt	nolueram nolueras noluerat nolueramus nolueratis noluerant

Notes:

1 Although these are called Irregular Verbs, they have many features in common with regular verbs:

   (a) the person endings;

   (b) -ra- in the imperfect of esse is not unlike -ba- in regular verbs;

   (c) -ro, -ris, -rit, etc. in the future of esse correspond to -bo, -bis, -bit, etc;

   (d) the perfect and pluperfect are regular.

2 Imperatives:
   es! este! (from esse)
   i! ite! (from ire)
   noli! nolite! (from nolle)
   posse and velle do not have imperatives

Section H: Numerals

	Cardinals	Ordinals
I	**unus, una, unum**, one	**primus, -a, -um**, first
II	**duo, duae, duo**, two	**secundus, -a, -um**, second
III	**tres, tres, tria**, three	**tertius, -a, -um**, third
IV	**quattuor**, four	**quartus, -a, -um**, fourth
V	**quinque**, five	**quintus, -a, -um**, fifth
VI	**sex**, six	**sextus, -a, -um**, sixth
VII	**septem**, seven	**septimus, -a, -um**, seventh
VIII	**octo**, eight	**octavus, -a, -um**, eighth
IX	**novem**, nine	**nonus, -a, -um**, ninth
X	**decem**, ten	**decimus, -a, -um**, tenth
XX	**viginti**, twenty	**vicesimus, -a, -um**, twentieth
L	**quinquaginta**, fifty	**quinquagesimus, -a, -um**, fiftieth
C	**centum**, hundred	**centesimus, -a, -um**, hundredth
D	**quingenti, -ae, -a**, five hundred	**quingentesimus, -a, -um**, five-hundredth
M	**mille**, a thousand	**millesimus, -a, -um**, thousandth

The ordinals have the same endings as **magnus, -a, -um**.

Of the above cardinals, only **unus, duo, tres** and **quingenti** have different endings for the cases:

	Masc.	Fem.	Neut.	Masc.	Fem.	Neut.	Masc.	Fem.	Neut.
Nom.	unus	una	unum	duo	duae	duo	tres	tres	tria
Acc.	unum	unam	unum	duos	duas	duo	tres	tres	tria
Gen.	unius	unius	unius	duorum	duarum	duorum	trium	trium	trium
Dat.	uni	uni	uni	duobus	duabus	duobus	tribus	tribus	tribus
Abl.	uno	una	uno	duobus	duabus	duobus	tribus	tribus	tribus

A Simplified Guide to Pronunciation

Consonants Most consonants are pronounced as in English, but the following should be noted:

> **b** before **s** or **t** is pronounced as English *p*: **urbs.**
> **c** is always hard and pronounced as English *k*: **cibus.**
> **g** is hard, as in English "get": **gemit.**
> **gn** in the middle of a word may be pronounced as the *ngn* in English "hangnail": **magnus.**
> **i** before a vowel is a consonant and pronounced as English *y*: **iānua.**
> **r** should be rolled: **rāmus.**
> **s** is pronounced as in English "sing," never as in "roses": **civis.**
> **t** is always hard as in "take", never soft as in "nation": **taceo.**
> **v** is pronounced as English *w*: **villa.**

Vowels and Diphthongs The following approximations are offered for the pronunciation of short and long vowels. In addition, long vowels should be held for a longer time than short ones.

SHORT	LONG
a = English "aha!" (first "a") (**pater**)	**ā** = English "aha!" (second "a") (**māter**)
e = English "pet" (**ego**)	**ē** = English "they" (**dēscendō**)
i = English "skit" (**iterum**)	**ī** = English "ski" (**īratus**)
o = English "for" (**omnēs**)	**ō** = English "holy" (**in hortō**)
u = English "put" (**ubi**)	**ū** = English "true" (**ūnus**)

The diphthong **ae** is pronounced as the *y* in English "sky" (**amicae**).
The diphthong **au** is pronounced as the *ow* in English "how" (**audit**).
The diphthong **ei** is pronounced as the *ay* in English "say" (**deinde**).

Stress Accent When Latin was spoken, certain syllables were stressed. The following is the general rule for deciding where the stress should fall:

(a) In a word of two syllables, the accent is on the first syllable, e.g. **ámō** and **ūnus.**

(b) In a word of more than two syllables,

    (i) the stress falls on the second last syllable if that syllable contains a long vowel or a short vowel followed by two consonants, e.g. **amātis** and **deféssus;**

    (ii) otherwise, the stress falls on the third last syllable, e.g. **celériter** and **sollícitus.**

Vocabulary

A

a, ab (+ *abl.*)	by, from
abeo, abire, abii, abitum	to go away
abhinc (+ *acc.*)	ago
absum, abesse, afui	to be away, be distant
accidit, accidere (3), **accidit**	to happen
accuso (1)	to accuse
accurro, accurrere (3), **accurri, accursum**	to run towards
ad (+ *acc.*)	to, at, near
adeo, adire, adii, aditum	to go towards
adhuc	still
adiuvo, adiuvare (1), **adiuvi, adiutum**	to help
advenio, advenire (4), **adveni, adventum**	to reach, arrive at
advesperascit, -ascere (3), **advesperavit**	evening is coming on, it is getting dark
aedificium, -i (*n*)	building
aestate	in summer
affero, afferre, attuli, allatum	to carry towards
age! agite!	come on!
ager, agri (*m*)	field
ago, agere (3), **egi, actum**	to do, drive
albatus, -a, -um	white
alius, alia, aliud	other, another
alter, altera, alterum	the other, the second
ambulo (1)	to walk
amica, -ae (*f*)	friend
amicus, -i (*m*)	friend
amo (1)	to like, love
amphitheatrum, -i (*n*)	amphitheatre
ancilla, -ae (*f*)	servant-girl
animal, animalis (*n*)	animal
animus, -i (*m*)	mind
in animo habere	to intend
annus, -i (*m*)	year
antea	previously, before
antiquus, -a, -um	ancient
aperio, aperire (4), **aperui, apertum**	to open
appareo (2)	to appear
appropinquo (1) (+ *dat.*)	to approach, draw near (to)
aqua, -ae (*f*)	water
arbor, arboris (*f*)	tree
arcus, -us (*m*)	arch
area, -ae (*f*)	yard, courtyard
arena, -ae (*f*)	arena, sand
arripio, arripere (3), **arripui, arreptum**	to snatch, seize
ars, artis (*f*)	skill, art
ascendo, ascendere (3), **ascendi, ascensum**	to climb up, go up
Asia, -ae (*f*)	Asia Minor
at	but
atque	and also
atrium, -i (*n*)	atrium, central room in a house
audio (4)	to hear, listen to
auriga, -ae (*m*)	charioteer
aurum, -i (*n*)	gold
aut ... aut ...	either ... or ...
auxilium, -i (*n*)	help

B

baculum, -i (*n*)	stick
bene	well
bona, bonorum (*n.pl*)	goods, possessions
bonus, -a, -um	good
bos, bovis (*m/f*)	ox, cow
brevis, brevis, breve	short

C

cado, cadere (3), **cecidi, casum**	to fall
calidus, -a, -um	warm
canis, canis (*m/f*)	dog
canto (1)	to sing
caput, capitis (*n*)	head
cauda, -ae (*f*)	tail
caupo, cauponis (*m*)	innkeeper
caupona, -ae (*f*)	inn
caveo, cavere (2), **cavi, cautum**	to watch out, be careful
celeriter	quickly
cena, -ae (*f*)	dinner

centum	hundred	deicio, deicere (3),	
cibus, -i (*m*)	food	deieci, deiectum	to throw down
Circus, -i (*m*)	Circus Maximus (a stadium in Rome)	descendo, descendere (3), descendi, descensum	to go down, climb down
cisium, -i (*n*)	light two-wheeled carriage	deus, -i (*m*)	god
cista, -ae (*f*)	trunk, box, chest	dico, dicere (3), dixi, dictum	to say, tell
civis, civis (*m*)	citizen	dies, diei (*m*)	day
clamo (1)	to shout	diligenter	carefully
clamor, clamoris (*m*)	a shout, shouting	discedo, discedere (3), discessi, discessum	to go away
claudo, claudere (3), clausi, clausum	to shut	diu	for a long time
cliens, clientis (*m*)	client, hanger-on	do, dare (1), dedi, datum	to give
cogito (1)	to think	doceo, docere (2), docui, doctum	to teach
complexus, -us (*m*)	embrace	doleo (2)	to be sorry
conduco, conducere (3), conduxi, conductum	to hire	domi	at home
conicio, conicere (3), conieci, coniectum	to throw	domina, -ae (*f*)	mistress
consido, considere (3), consedi, consessum	to sit down	dominus, -i (*m*)	master, owner
conspicio, conspicere (3), conspexi, conspectum	to catch sight of	domo	from home
		domus, -us (*f*)	house, home
		dormio (4)	to sleep
constituo, constituere (3), constitui, constitutum	to decide	duco, ducere (3), duxi, ductum	to lead, take
consulo, consulere (3), consului, consultum	to consult	dum	while
		duo, duae, duo	two
convoco (1)	to call together		
corpus, corporis (*n*)	body	**E**	
cras	tomorrow	e, ex (+ *abl.*)	from, out of
cubiculum, -i (*n*)	bedroom	ecce!	look! look at!
cubitum ire	to go to bed	effero, efferre, extuli, elatum,	to carry out
culpa, -ae (*f*)	fault, blame	effugio, effugere (3), effugi	to escape, run away
cum (+ *abl.*)	with		
cuncti, -ae, -a	all	ego	I
cur?	why?	eheu!	alas!
Curia, -ae (*f*)	Senate-house	eius	his, her
curo (1)	to look after	emo, emere (3), emi, emptum	to buy
curro, currere (3), cucurri, cursum	to run	enim	for
		eo, ire, ivi, itum	to go
custodio (4)	to guard	epistola, -ae (*f*)	letter
custos, custodis (*m*)	guard	equus, -i (*m*)	horse
		eram	I was
D		erro (1)	to wander
de (+ *abl.*)	down from, concerning	esse	to be
decem	ten	esurio (4)	to be hungry
decimus, -a, -um	tenth	et	and
defessus, -a, -um	tired		

etiam	also, even
eugepae!	well done! hurray!
excito (1)	to waken
exclamo (1)	to exclaim, shout out
exeo, exire, exii, exitum	to go out
explico (1)	to explain
exspecto (1)	to wait for
extendo, extendere (3), **extendi, extentum**	to hold out
extra (+ *acc.*)	outside
extraho, extrahere (3), **extraxi, extractum**	to drag out

F

fabula, -ae (*f*)	story
facio, facere (3), **feci, factum**	to make, do
fatuus, -a, -um	stupid
feriae, -arum (*f.pl*)	holidays
feriatus, -a, -um	on holiday
fero, ferre, tuli, latum	to carry, bring
ferociter	fiercely
festino (1)	to hurry
fidelis, -is, -e	faithful
filia, -ae (*f*)	daughter
filius, -i (*m*)	son
finio (4)	to finish
fortasse	perhaps
forum, -i (*n*)	the Forum (town centre of Rome), market
fossa, -ae (*f*)	ditch
fragor, fragoris (*m*)	noise, din, crash
frater, fratris (*m*)	brother
frigidus, -a, -um	cold
frustra	in vain
fugio, fugere (3), **fugi, fugitum**	to flee
fui	I have been, I was (perfect of **esse**)
furtim	stealthily

G

gaudeo (2)	to rejoice
gemo, gemere (3), **gemui, gemitum**	to groan
gero, gerere (3), **gessi, gestum**	to wear
gloria, -ae (*f*)	fame, glory
Graecus, -a, -um	Greek

H

habeo (2)	to have, hold
habito (1)	to live
haereo, haerere (2), **haesi, haesum**	to stick
hic, haec, hoc	this
hic (*adverb*)	here
hodie	today
homo, hominis (*m*)	man, person
hora, -ae (*f*)	hour
hortus, -i (*m*)	garden
hospes, hospitis (*m*)	friend, guest
hostis, hostis (*m*)	enemy
huic	dative of **hic**
huius	genitive of **hic**

I

iaceo (2)	to lie down
iam	now, already
ianitor, ianitoris (*m*)	doorkeeper
ianua, -ae (*f*)	door
ibi	there
idem, eadem, idem	the same
identidem	repeatedly
igitur	therefore
ignavus, -a, -um	lazy, cowardly
ille, illa, illud	that; he, she, it
immobilis, -is, -e	motionless
impedio (4)	to hinder
impono, imponere (3), **imposui, impositum**	to place upon
in (+ *abl.*)	in, on
in (+ *acc.*)	into
induo, induere (3), **indui, indutum**	to put on
infirmus, -a, -um	weak, shaky
ingens, ingentis	huge
inquit	(he/she) says, said
inspicio, inspicere (3), **inspexi, inspectum**	to examine
intra (+ *acc.*)	inside
intro (1)	to enter
invenio, invenire (4), **inveni, inventum**	to find, come upon
invito (1)	to invite
invitus, -a, -um	unwilling, unwillingly
ipse, ipsa, ipsum	-self
ira, -ae (*f*)	anger
iratus, -a, -um	angry
ire	see **eo**

irrumpo, irrumpere (3),
  irrupi, irruptum — to burst in
is, ea, id — he, she, it; that
ita — in this way
ita vero! — yes
Italia, -ae (*f*) — Italy
itaque — and so, therefore
iter, itineris (*n*) — journey, road
iterum — again, a second time
iubeo, iubere (2), iussi,
  iussum — to order, bid, tell

L

labor, laboris (*m*) — work, toil
laboro (1) — to work
lacrimo (1) — to weep, cry
laetus, -a, -um — happy, glad
lavo, lavare (1), lavi,
  lavatum — to wash
lectica, -ae (*f*) — litter
lecticarius, -i (*m*) — litter-bearer
lectus, -i (*m*) — bed, couch
legatus, -i (*m*) — envoy
lego, legere (3), legi,
  lectum — to read
lente — slowly
liber, libri (*m*) — book
liberi, -orum (*m.pl*) — children
licet (2) — it is allowed
longus, -a, -um — long
ludi, -orum (*m.pl*) — games
ludo, ludere (3), lusi,
  lusum — to play
lupus, -i (*m*) — wolf
lux, lucis (*f*) — light
  prima luce — at dawn

M

magnus, -a, -um — large, great, loud
  (of voice)
mandatum, -i (*n*) — instruction
mane — in the morning, early
maneo, manere (2),
  mansi, mansum — to remain, stay
mango, mangonis (*m*) — slave-dealer
manus, -us (*f*) — hand
mater, matris (*f*) — mother
me — me
medius, -a, -um — mid-, middle of
  media nox — midnight

melior, melioris — better
mercator,
  mercatoris (*m*) — merchant
meridies, -ei (*m*) — mid-day
meta, -ae (*f*) — turning-post (in Circus)
meus, -a, -um — my, mine
mihi — to me, for me
miles, militis (*m*) — soldier
mille (*pl.* milia) — thousand
minime! — not at all, not in the
  least, no!
mirus, -a, -um — wonderful, strange
miser, misera, miserum — unhappy, wretched
  o me miserum! — poor me! O dear me!
mitto, mittere (3), misi,
  missum — to send
molestus, -a, -um — troublesome, annoying
mons, montis (*m*) — mountain, hill
mors, mortis (*f*) — death
mortuus, -a, -um — dead
mos, moris (*m*) — custom
moveo, movere (2),
  movi, motum — to move
mox — soon, presently
mulier, mulieris (*f*) — woman
multi, -ae, -a — many
multitudo, -tudinis (*f*) — crowd
murmur, murmuris (*n*) — rumble
murus, -i (*m*) — wall
mus, muris (*m*) — mouse
musso (1) — to murmur, mutter

N

nam — for
narro (1) — to tell (a story)
nato (1) — to swim
-ne — (indicates a question)
Neapolis, -is (*f*) — Naples
necesse — necessary
neco (1) — to kill
nemo — no one
neque — and . . . not
  neque . . . neque . . . — neither . . . nor
nihil — nothing
nil — nothing
nisi — unless, if . . . not
nobis — to us, for us
nocturnus, -a, -um — happening during the
  night

noli (+ *inf.*)!	do not . . . !	pervenio, pervenire (4),	
nolo, nolle, nolui	to be unwilling, refuse	perveni, perventum	to arrive at, reach
nomen, nominis (*n*)	name	pes, pedis (*m*)	foot
non	not	peto, petere (3), petivi,	to seek, aim at, make
nondum	not yet	petitum	for, ask
nonne?	surely?	pictura, -ae (*f*)	picture
nos	we, us	piscina, -ae (*f*)	fishpond
noster, nostra, nostrum	our	plaustrum, -i (*n*)	wagon, cart
novem	nine	plenus, -a, -um	full
novus, -a, -um	new	pluit (3)	it rains
nox, noctis (*f*)	night	pono, ponere (3), posui,	
nullus, -a, -um	no, none	positum	to place, put
numerus, -i (*m*)	number	porta, -ae (*f*)	gate
numquam	never	porto (1)	to carry
nunc	now	possum, posse, potui	to be able
nuntius, -i (*m*)	messenger	post (+ *acc.*)	after
		postquam	after

O

obdormio (4)	to fall asleep	praecedo, praecedere (3), praecessi, praecessum	to go in front
obesus, -a, -um	fat	praeclarus, -a, -um	famous
occupatus, -a, -um	busy	praedo, praedonis (*m*)	robber
occurro, -currere (3), -curri, -cursum (+ *dat.*)	to meet	prasinus, -a, -um	green
		prima luce	at dawn
octo	eight	primus, -a, -um	first
oculus, -i (*m*)	eye	princeps, principis (*m*)	emperor
olim	once upon a time	procedo, procedere (3), processi, processum	to go forward
oliva, -ae (*f*)	olive	procul	far, far off
olivetum, -i (*n*)	olive-grove	promitto, promittere (3), promisi, promissum	to promise
omnis, -is, -e	every, all		
onus, oneris (*n*)	burden, load	prope (+ *acc.*)	near
orator, oratoris (*m*)	orator, speaker	puella, -ae (*f*)	girl
os, ossis (*n*)	bone	puer, pueri (*m*)	boy
		pulvis, pulveris (*m*)	dust

P

paratus, -a, -um	prepared, ready	punio (4)	to punish
parens, parentis (*m/f*)	parent	purus, -a, -um	spotless, clean
paro (1)	to prepare		

Q

pars, partis (*f*)	part	qualis?	of what kind?
parvulus, -a, -um	small, little, tiny	quamquam	although
parvus, -a, -um	small	quando?	when?
pater, patris (*m*)	father	quattuor	four
patruus, -i (*m*)	uncle	qui, quae, quod	who, which
paulisper	for a short time	quidam, quaedam, quoddam	a, a certain
pecunia, -ae (*f*)	money		
per (+ *acc.*)	through, along	quiesco, quiescere (3), quievi, quietum	to rest
periculosus, -a, -um	dangerous		
periculum, -i (*n*)	danger	quinque	five
pernocto (1)	to spend the night		
perterritus, -a, -um	terrified		

quis? quid?	who? what?	**se**	himself, herself, itself, themselves
quo?	whither? where (to)?	**secundus, -a, -um**	second
quod	because	**sed**	but
quod	see **qui, quae, quod**	**sedeo, sedere** (2), **sedi, sessum**	to sit
quomodo?	how?	**semisomnus, -a, -um**	half-asleep
quoque	also	**semper**	always
quot?	how many?	**senator, senatoris** (*m*)	senator
		senatus, -us (*m*)	senate
R		**septem**	seven
raeda, -ae (*f*)	coach, carriage	**septimus, -a, -um**	seventh
raedarius, -i (*m*)	coachman, driver	**sepulcrum, -i** (*n*)	tomb
ramus, -i (*m*)	branch	**sero**	late
raro	seldom	**servo** (1)	to save
redeo, redire, redii, reditum	to return, go back	**servus, -i** (*m*)	slave
relinquo, relinquere (3), **reliqui, relictum**	to leave	**sex**	six
repello, repellere (3), **reppuli, repulsum**	to drive off, drive back	**si**	if
		sibi	to himself, to themselves
reprehendo, -hendere (3), **-hendi, -hensum**	to scold, blame	**silentium, -i** (*n*)	silence
res, rei (*f*)	thing	**silva, -ae** (*f*)	wood
respondeo, respondere (2), **respondi, responsum**	to reply	**simul**	at the same time
		sine (+ *abl.*)	without
revoco (1)	to call back	**soleo** (2)	to be accustomed, in the habit of
rideo, ridere (2), **risi, risum**	to smile, laugh	**sollicitus, -a, -um**	worried
rimosus, -a, -um	full of cracks, leaky	**solus, -a, -um**	alone
ripa, -ae (*f*)	bank (of a river)	**somnium, -i** (*n*)	dream
rivus, -i (*m*)	stream	**sonitus, -us** (*m*)	sound
rogo (1)	to ask	**sordidus, -a, -um**	dirty
Roma, -ae (*f*)	Rome	**soror, sororis** (*f*)	sister
Romanus, -a, -um	Roman	**specto** (1)	to look at
rota, -ae (*f*)	wheel	**spina, -ae** (*f*)	backbone, central barrier
russatus, -a, -um	red	**statim**	immediately
		statua, -ae (*f*)	statue
S		**stercus, stercoris** (*n*)	dung
saepe	often	**sto, stare** (1), **steti, statum**	to stand
saluto (1)	to greet, welcome	**stola, -ae** (*f*)	stola (a woman's over-garment)
salve! salvete!	greetings! welcome!	**strenue**	strenuously, hard
salvus, -a, -um	safe	**strenuus, -a, -um**	active, busy
satis	enough	**sub** (+ *abl.*)	under, beneath
scaena, -ae (*f*)	scene	**subito**	suddenly
scelestus, -a, -um	wicked	**sumo, sumere** (3), **sumpsi, sumptum**	to take, pick up
scio, scire (4), **scivi, scitum**	to know	**supra** (+ *acc.*)	above
scribo, scribere (3), **scripsi, scriptum**	to write	**surgo, surgere** (3), **surrexi, surrectum**	to rise

suus, -a, -um	his, her, its, their (own)
T	
tabellarius, -i (*m*)	courier
taberna, -ae (*f*)	shop
taceo (2)	to be silent
tacite	silently
talis, -is, -e	like this, of this kind
tam	so
tamen	however, nevertheless
tandem	at last, at length
tantum	only
tarde	slowly
tardus, -a, -um	slow
temerarius, -a, -um	rash, reckless, bold
tempto (1)	to try
tempus, temporis (*n*)	time
teneo (2)	to hold
terra, -ae (*f*)	earth, ground
terreo (2)	to terrify, frighten
tibi	to you, for you
timeo (2)	to fear, be afraid
timidus, -a, -um	afraid
toga, -ae (*f*)	toga
totus, -a, -um	all, the whole
trado, tradere (3), tradidi, traditum	to hand over
traho, trahere (3), traxi, tractum	to drag, pull
trans (+ *acc.*)	across
transeo, transire, transii, transitum	to cross
tremo, tremere (3), tremui	to tremble
tres, tres, tria	three
Troia, -ae (*f*)	Troy
tu	you
tunica, -ae (*f*)	tunic
turba, -ae (*f*)	crowd, mob
tuus, -a, -um	your
U	
ubi	when, where

unus, -a, -um	one
urbs, urbis (*f*)	city
uxor, uxoris (*f*)	wife
V	
valde	very much, very
vale! valete!	goodbye!
vehiculum, -i (*n*)	vehicle
velle	see **volo**
venetus, -a, -um	blue
venio, venire (4), veni, ventum	to come
verbero (1)	to beat, whip
verbosus, -a, -um	talkative
verbum, -i (*n*)	word
vestigium, -i (*n*)	trace, footprint
veto, vetare (1), vetui, vetitum	to forbid
vexo (1)	to annoy
via, -ae (*f*)	road, street
viator, viatoris (*m*)	traveller
vicinus, -a, -um	neighbouring, adjacent
victor, victoris (*m*)	conqueror, victor
video, videre (2), vidi, visum	to see
videri	to seem
videtur	he/she/it seems
vigilo (1)	to be watchful, stay awake
vilicus, -i (*m*)	foreman, overseer
villa, -ae (*f*)	country house, farm
vinea, -ae (*f*)	vineyard
vinum, -i (*n*)	wine
vir, viri (*m*)	man
virga, -ae (*f*)	stick
vis (vim, vi) (*f*)	force
visito (1)	to visit
vito (1)	to avoid
vobis	to you, for you
volo, velle, volui	to wish
vos	you
vox, vocis (*f*)	voice
vult	(he/she) wishes, wants

Solutions

Unit I, page *9*:

¹C	²E	³S	Q	U	⁴I	⁵S	
L	⁷T	U	U	S	N	⁸A	
⁹A	¹⁰R	B	O	¹¹R	E	¹²M	
¹³M	A	N	¹⁴E	¹⁵I	T	A	
¹⁶A	¹⁷M	A	U	D	I	S	
¹⁸T	U	¹⁹E	²⁰M	E	A	²¹M	
²²A	²³M	²⁴A	N	T	²⁵M	E	
²⁶D	U	²⁷M	T	O	G	A	

Unit II, page *15*:

¹S		²H		³S	U	R	G	⁴I	S			⁵A
⁶A	M	A	S					N				G
L		B		⁷S	P	⁸E	C	T	A	⁹S	N	E
V		E		U		X		R		E		
E		M		R		I		¹⁰A	U	D	I	¹¹T
		U		G		T		S		E		I
	¹²E	S	T	I	S		¹³N			N		M
¹⁴E	S			M		¹⁵M	A	N	¹⁶E	T		E
	¹⁷S	U	M	U	S		T		S			S
	E			S		¹⁸P	O	R	T	A	S	

Unit III, page *21*:

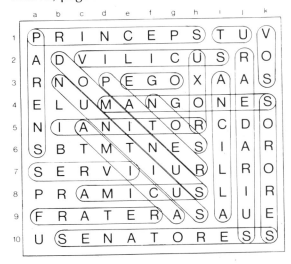

	a	b	c	d	e	f	g	h	i	j	k
1	P	R	I	N	C	E	P	S	T	U	V
2	A	D	V	I	L	I	C	U	S	R	O
3	R	N	O	P	E	G	O	X	A	A	S
4	E	L	U	M	A	N	G	O	N	E	S
5	N	I	A	N	I	T	O	R	C	D	O
6	S	B	T	M	T	N	E	S	I	A	R
7	S	E	R	V	I	I	U	R	L	R	O
8	P	R	A	M	I	C	U	S	L	I	R
9	F	R	A	T	E	R	A	S	A	U	E
10	U	S	E	N	A	T	O	R	E	S	S

Unit IV, pages *28–9*:

¹I	²R	³A	⁴T	⁵I	⁶C	⁷I	V	I	S
⁸N	O	S	A	⁹S	¹⁰U	R	B	¹¹S	¹²P
¹³I	T	¹⁴A	R	¹⁵M	R	E	¹⁶Q	U	O
¹⁸R	A	E	D	A	R	¹⁹I	U	M	R
E	R	²⁰M	A	N	E	B	A	²¹N	T
²²A	U	D	²³I	E	B	A	S	²⁵E	A
R	²⁶M	E	T	²⁷T	A	N	²⁸T	²⁹U	M
³⁰T	A	C	E	N	T	³¹T	E	N	³³E
E	³⁴P	E	R	³⁵O	N	E	R	A	G
³⁷E	U	M	³⁸I	N	F	I	R	M	O

The Riddle of the Sphinx:

The answer is "a man", because in his early life as an infant he crawls on hands and knees; in the middle part of his life he walks upright; and in his declining years he is an old man walking with a stick.

Unit V, page 35:

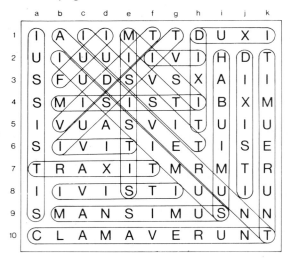

Unit VI, page 41:

Unit VII, page 46:

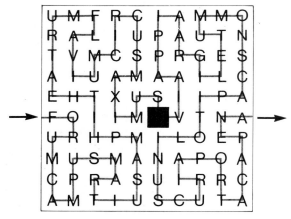

Unit VIII, page 54:

What's Wrong Here?

page 47:

1 TV aerial
2 Too many windows in outside wall of building
3 Modern street lamp
4 Modern shop front
5 Street name on wall
6 Clock over shop doorway
7 **Raeda** in the street during daylight hours
8 Modern pneumatic tyre on **raeda**
9 Bicycle
10 Bowler hat

11 Umbrella
12 Modern book
13 Training shoes
14 Romans used neither street numbers nor Arabic numerals
15 Arabic numerals; BC date makes no sense
16 Adult wearing a **bulla**
17 Modern kettle
18 Drinking fountain
19 Spectacles
20 Wristwatch